Writing Well
Creative Writing and Mental Health

*Deborah Philips, Liz Linington
and Debra Penman*

Jessica Kingsley Publishers
London and Philadelphia

The right of Deborah Philips, Liz Linington and Debra Penman to be identified as authors of this work has been asserted by them in accordance with the Copyright, Designs and Patents Act 1988.
First Published in the United Kingdom in 1999 by
Jessica Kingsley Publishers Ltd,
116 Pentonville Road, London N1 9JB,
England
and
325 Chestnut Street,
Philadelphia PA 19106, USA
www.jkp.com

© Copyright 1999 Deborah Philips, Liz Linington and Debra Penman

Library of Congress Cataloging in Publication Data
Philips, Deborah, 1954
Writing well: creative writing and mental health / Deborah Philips, Liz Linington, and Debra Penman.
p. cm. Includes bibliographical references and index.
ISBN 1 85302 650 6 (alk. paper)
1. Creative writing – Therapeutic use – Handbook, manuals, etc.
2. Self-actualization (Psychology) – Handbooks, manuals etc.
3. Creative writing – Therapeutic use. I. Linington, Liz, 1969 II. Penman, Debra. III. Title.
RC489.W75P48 1998
616.89'165–dc21
98-41232
CIP

British Library Cataloguing in Publication Data
Philips, Deborah
Writing well : creative writing and mental health
1.Creative writing - Therapeutic use
I.Title II.Penman, Debra III.Linington, Liz
614.8'516'0874

Printed and Bound in Great Britain by
Athenaeum Press, Gateshead, Tyne and Wear

Writing Well

of related interest

The Self on the Page
Theory and Practice of Creative Writing in Personal Development
Edited by Celia Hunt and Fiona Sampson
ISBN 1 85302 470 8 pb
ISBN 1 85302 469 4 hb

Writing Myself
The Therapeutic Potential of Creative Writing
Gillie Bolton
ISBN 1 85302 599 2 pb

Contents

ACKNOWLEDGEMENTS 8

FOREWORD 9

1. Introduction   13

2. Warm-Up Exercises   39

3. Beginnings   45

4. Introductory Work   53

5. Memories   57

6. Empathy   77

7. Changes and Endings   85

8. Imagined Worlds   89

9. Opening Up   97

10. General Themes   109

11. Exploring Literary Form   117

APPENDIX 1 GUIDELINES FOR DEVELOPING
AND ADAPTING YOUR OWN EXERCISES   125

APPENDIX 2 CREATIVE WRITING BOOKS
(OR WHY THIS BOOK IS NECESSARY)   129

APPENDIX 3 USEFUL ORGANISATIONS   135

THE AUTHORS   139

REFERENCES   141

SUBJECT INDEX   143

AUTHOR INDEX   149

For Alfred Linington, Stan Penman and Klaus Philips

Acknowledgements

Thanks are due to Rose Atfield and to Sharon MacDonald who read and commented on the manuscript, and to Giles, and especially to Barry Palmer; to the DUET (Development of University Teaching) Literary Practice Group, and to all those who have helped in the running of the groups: Alex, Darlene, Jane, Jess, Marie. Special thanks to Garry Whannel, Tim Barritt, Joe Barritt-Clarke, Peter Horah, Paula Baker, Vicky Morgan, Sally Newton and Dinah Penman for their support, and to Ed Brennan, Kevin Gallagher, Gill Howard for checking the manuscript.

Thanks are mostly due, however, to all the members of the writing groups at St Charles Acute Adult Day Hospital, especially Norman, who were the first to test this work out, and who taught us a great deal.

Foreword

This project emerged from the experience of running a creative writing group at St Charles Acute Adult Day Hospital in West London. In response to a demand from clients for such a group, we – one academic who had some experience of teaching creative writing in student groups, and two occupational therapists who had some experience of creative writing groups in a variety of mental health contexts – started one.

We discovered from the few books on creative writing that were available to us in the hospital that many of the exercises which are frequently used in creative writing groups were simply not appropriate for a group within the context of a psychiatric unit. They could be too threatening, too challenging, or simply assumed experiences which our clients had not shared. Checking reference libraries for work on creative writing in a mental health context, we found that there was very little that was appropriate to the needs of our groups. Between us, therefore, we devised a structured way of working with our own writing groups, adapting standard creative writing exercises from other sources (such as creative writing handbooks for students) and eventually devising our own. We have not intentionally used material here from other people, but we do recognise that our own practice has been informed by a range of sources, and can only apologise if we have not acknowledged them.

The function of this group was not in any way conceived as interpretative, but rather as a means of facilitating self-expression. A creative writing group can be seen as therapeutic in much the same way as other forms of creative activities can be – that the act of producing something can in itself be beneficial. Of course, what people write *is* open to interpretation, but we very much felt that the idea that what was written might be seen as subject to interpretation could be construed as inhibiting and therefore constraining to the practice of writing. We would, however, often discuss the implications of the work and the use that individual members made of the group in our feedback to one another and, if it was felt necessary, to a staff feedback session or supervisor. While it is important to sustain confidentiality within the group, there are occasions when a piece of writing can indicate a problem that requires immediate intervention, such as a suicidal ideation that may not have been apparent before. In these rare circumstances, we felt it important to reserve the right to discuss material from the group professionally.

This book is very much about what we learned from our experience. The exercises included are all tried and tested with our own groups: some of them worked and some of them proved less engaging, in which cases we have tried to identify why they didn't work, and adjusted them accordingly.

How to use this book

The exercises are divided into sections (each comprising a chapter), each of which addresses particular themes or is appropriate to a particular stage in the group. Each exercise indicates the materials needed (most sessions do not require anything other than pens and paper), and a recommended warm-up exercise. Each exercise is also accompanied by notes which suggest issues that might need consideration in the context of your own group. There is no need to abide by these recommendations, or the wording that we have used in the exercises. There is a section which indicates means of devising your own exercises in the appendices, and a chapter of introductory warm-up exercises (Chapter 2) which offers a few alternatives to the warm-ups we have recommended for each exercise.

The structure of the exercises are also open to adaptation. Although we have found that a regular and a familiar structure can be beneficial to people's writing, and provides a secure framework within which to write, no exercise depends on the five points we have outlined. The section entitled 'Finally' attached to each exercise allows you to prolong or curtail a writing exercise, and it is perfectly feasible to cut out one of the stages if the group has spent too much time on other stages, or, alternatively, to add another if the group is clearly not inspired by the stages that you have outlined. The language in which we have expressed the exercises is not fixed either – it is important that you express each stage of the task in language that feels appropriate to you and to the context of the group, and that you adapt the instructions to your own requirements. For some sessions you might prefer to begin from some introductory comments, and allow the group to write without specific directions from you, and as the group grows in confidence, its members may well begin to initiate their own ideas for themes and sessions.

It is perfectly possible to work through the sections consecutively, but you may find that too many exercises of one kind can become repetitive, and that the group will react negatively to an unbroken succession of exercises that focus on positive or negative feelings or on concrete or abstract themes. Instead, we would recommend that you be sensitive to the mood of the group, and to judge its own rhythms. From this knowledge, you can choose from the sections which address particular themes or concerns appropriate to the needs of your own group at any particular stage in its development.

If a particular member of the group is having difficulty engaging with the rest of the group, it is important to choose a task that will involve them. Knowledge about individuals will emerge over the course of the life of the group, and it is relatively easy to find an exercise that engages with their concerns. The notes appended to each exercise suggest points to consider to ensure that everyone in the group is included. There are a few exercises which urge caution, and which you should consider carefully in relation to your own group; these are pointed to in the notes, and some are specifically flagged as requiring special consideration. These few exercises need particular care and attention and may not be appropriate for your own situation, these are marked with an 'NB' at the beginning, and should be considered in the light of your knowledge of the group and its membership.

How you work with this book depends entirely on the group of people you are working with – every exercise should be tailored in terms of your own client group. Each individual will arrive in the group with their unique history and set of experiences, and you must be aware of the issues of difference within your group. Be sensitive to the differences of age, race, class, gender and sexuality that will be present in any group, and allow space and leeway within the exercises and the discussion to take account of these differences. In selecting and in setting up any exercise, it is important to assess the experience of the members of your own group, and to ensure that the exercise does not make any unwarranted assumptions about the group members, or exclude any of them. Your knowledge of the individuals within your own group is central to this, and in most cases, it is simple to make adjustments that will include everyone. The notes at the end of each exercise should, on the whole, alert facilitators to any potential problems.

As a group facilitator, you must also be alert to more pragmatic considerations. In presenting a writing task, you need to consider whether it can be assumed that the experience it is concerned with has been available to everyone in the group. A group member will feel isolated and alienated if the task requires memories and experience that exclude them. These awarenesses should inform both your choice of exercise and also the way in which the writing exercises are structured – it is your own knowledge of and sensitivity to the group that will make it successful and productive.

We sometimes discovered in our own groups that an original idea for an exercise had to be modified in the light of resistances to writing on the part of the group; this usually emerged because there were responses that we had not anticipated, and because we had not gauged the potential reactions sufficiently thoroughly. We have attempted here to restructure the exercises in the light of these responses, but there may still be assumptions here that we have not recognised in ourselves.

Writing can inadvertently reveal things about people that they had not anticipated, and it is necessary to be prepared for potential vulnerabilities and conflicts within the group. Writing can reveal unexpected things about people, and change the group's perceptions about any of the members. One of the most valuable things that we have found to emerge from all the different writing groups we have been involved with is the mutual support that its members give to one another.

CHAPTER I

Introduction

This is not a book about writing well. There are many books available for those who wish to explore their creative potential in writing and to experiment with language and literary form – this is not one of them. There are any number of creative writing handbooks and writing workshops which are there to advise and instruct on how to use one's life experience to improve one's writing, but this is a book that is about using writing to promote a sense of well-being.

The majority of creative writing handbooks (some of which are listed in the 'Useful books' section in Appendix 2) are written for those who already have some confidence in their writing ability and who are prepared to take risks. This is by no means the case for those who are, for whatever reason, in a vulnerable state or crisis situation. This is a book for those who are professionally working with such people, and is intended for creative writing groups in which the practice of writing is primarily for its therapeutic benefits, rather than for the production of elegant poetry and prose.

This handbook has grown out of our own experiences in work with psychiatric patients in a range of different institutions, and although it is not restricted to use in a mental health context, it has been designed with that specifically in mind.

Why writing can help

When people are in a state of great distress, or in a great depression, they may feel that they have nothing good in their lives. Writing is a means of evoking positive memories and of enabling the production of something valuable from the imagination, which can provoke appreciation from other group members. Writing is also a means of articulating difficult feelings and unhappy memories, and transmuting them into a form that makes them possible to confront. Writing is one of the easiest means of allowing people to recognise that they have abilities and the means to produce interesting and creative work within themselves; it requires very few resources, and is an activity within the experience of most people. But the particular advantage of writing is that participants can choose to write whatever they want – the production of something beautiful or useful has not been demanded, and difficult and unacceptable ideas can be transformed into a form that can be appreciated and explored.

At one level, writing can act in the same way as other forms of creative activities which explore self-expression through a particular medium, in that group members can produce something of which they may be proud and an experience which they can take away from the group. There are many whose skills and enthusiasms do not lie in the visual arts or in music, movement or drama, and who would benefit from an opportunity to express themselves in a different medium. Some people will have a strong affinity to the written word, and can find it the most appropriate means of exploring their feelings. Writing in a therapeutic context can also be used to complement work in other groups and disciplines, as Lauer and Goldfield (1970, p.251) discovered in their research:

> Besides the patients' desires for self-expression, another factor enhancing the value of creative writing was the concurrent use of other forms of therapy. Reciprocally, creative writing seemed to enhance other forms of psychotherapy.

Writing is also one of the easiest skills to develop outside an institution, there are a great many local writing groups which can be recommended to group members who have moved beyond the confines of a therapeutic writing group. Creative writing can therefore act as a positive means of transition from a therapeutic context into an everyday practice, and enables skills that may have been developed within an institution to be employed outside its constraints. There are a now number of creative writing groups which have been specifically set up by writers with the experience of mental health institutions (see Appendix 3, 'Useful organisations').

Writers themselves have always known that there are therapeutic benefits to be derived from the process of writing. Shakespeare, Keats, Virginia Woolf and Alice Walker are only some of the best-known names who have framed their mental distress into a literary form and who have remarked upon the beneficial aspects of the process. Freud (1908, p.131) credits the poet with a recognition of the unconscious long before his own academic theorisation of the concept, and acknowledges that the poet or writer has access to insights that escape the ordinary mortal:

> We layman have always been intensely curious to know... from what sources that strange being the creative writer draws his material, and how he manages to make such an impression on us with it and to arouse in us emotions of which, perhaps, we had not even thought ourselves capable.

It is in that challenge to expected responses that the processes of writing can be so therapeutically valuable, whether or not the writer produces something that is of abiding literary value. For Freud, the writer is a special kind of being, despite the creativity that he uncovered in his own and in his patients' dreams. A creative writer, however, need not be a special category of person (or even a man). Laymen and women too (as Freud knew only too well) can experience the curious feeling that he describes of not recognising where it is that the material they produce comes from, and also of writing things of which they would not have thought themselves capable.

Since Freud, a wealth of writers' groups from different communities have challenged any such notion of the special status of the writer and, since the 1960s, feminist writing groups and radical publishers have compounded that challenge in their assertion that everyone has an important story to tell (see, for example, Cadman, Chester and Pivot 1981 for an account of feminist printing and publishing). Creative writing groups and publishing companies dedicated to publishing alternative stories have flourished since the 1960s in Britain and America (see Worpole 1984 for an account of the development of community writing) and have enabled a great range of 'ordinary' people to find some extraordinary voices. As one woman member of a creative writing workshop for the elderly has expressed it:

> the writing workshop allows... lives to 'come to the writing'; allows us to hear the testimony of the silent ones: the songs, tales, superstitions, life stories of the furriers, 'operators by blouses', survivors of two World Wars, the housewives, ordinary working women, ordinary working men, the many remarkable people among them... (Margaret Friedman, quoted in Kaminsky 1987, p.71)

The writing of ordinary people can be deeply affecting, and arouse emotions and memories that are of importance both to themselves and to others. It is a frequent experience of creative writing groups that participants will react to a piece of their own work with the exclamation: 'I didn't know that I thought that!' The experience of reading something that one has written in print also has a similar quality of distance from the known self and its capabilities. As many writers know, the act of writing in itself can shape a thought or idea; as the writer Julia Casterton (1986, p.5) puts it:

> Words come out differently on paper to how we imagine them in our heads. We discover ourselves through the form of the sentence. The act of transforming our knots into marks on the paper begins to give a discipline. Something inside says 'You can't say it that way, it doesn't work', and so we change it. Even as we start to write, we find ourselves making contact with feelings for rhythm and style.

Writing as therapy

Creative writing is now generally recognised by many mental health professionals as an important and valuable component in a therapeutic plan, and can often be an established practice in hospitals, prisons and other forms of therapeutic community. 'Poetry therapy' has been known in America since the 1950s – there is even an American Academy of Poetry Therapy (see Alice Glarden Brand's 'The uses of writing in psychotherapy' in Glarden Brand 1981 for an account of the development of creative writing as a therapeutic practice). The American Psychiatric Association recommended in 1980 that 'Mental health professionals who hope to offer a full range of treatment should have at least a basic understanding of the creative arts therapies' (Morrison 1987, p.22).

There are a number of observable and recognised clinical and practical benefits that can derive from the practice of creative writing, although research in this area currently remains limited. The following are among those we have observed in our own groups.

1. Writing provides an opportunity to externalise feelings

Participation in a creative writing group allows for the expression of feelings, both positive and negative. Among the functions of writing is that it requires the writer to articulate feelings about themselves and others in a form, and that form can give shape to what might otherwise be chaotic thoughts and ideas. The shaping of ideas into a formal piece of prose or poetry can allow the writer some distance from their thoughts, and enables them to be put into a different perspective. The practice of expressing ideas and feelings in a relatively unfamiliar form can allow for the development of new insights. As American psychiatrist Adam Blatner has put it: 'Employing a number of unfamiliar metaphors, such as can be found in poetry or art, dance or drama, the patient finds ways of expressing the nuances of personal feelings' (Preface to Morrison 1987, p.19).

The use of imaginative work can be relatively unthreatening and so enables the articulation of difficult or contradictory ideas – the creative writer is not being clinically assessed as they may be in other contexts within an institution. Creative writing can therefore offer a relatively safe form of expression for dangerous and difficult emotions, and so facilitate their exploration.

2. Writing promotes trust and a sense of community

Writing can be an intensely personal experience, and conditions of trust are integral to the group. A stress on confidentiality within the group is vital to this promotion of trust. As Freud noted (1908, p.133), in adulthood there are very few opportunities for sharing the daydreams and fantasies that it once was possible to express in childhood games:

> The adult is ashamed of his phantasies and hides them from other people. He cherishes his phantasies as his most intimate possessions, and as a rule he would rather confess his misdeeds than tell anyone his phantasies. It may come about that for that reason he believes he is the only person who invents such phantasies and has no idea that creations of this kind are widespread among other people.

A creative writing group offers a means of providing a safe space in which to articulate intimate thoughts and feelings which the writer may feel are childish or embarrassing. The group nature of the activity allows participants to recognise that such thoughts are indeed widespread, in allowing themselves to express them to others and in hearing other people articulate ideas that are shared. The sharing of written work is in itself a means of promoting social interaction, and of encouraging group members into a sense of community. The experience of a shared endeavour can in itself promote positive feelings and a sense of cohesion.

3. Writing can prompt reminiscence

According to Freud, painful memories are never forgotten. The act of writing can both prompt memories and allow for their expression in a manageable form. The empathy of others which the act of sharing these memories can provoke is often one of the most rewarding parts of membership of the group. The group offers a safe forum in which difficult memories which may not have previously been articulated, or only articulated in a one to one context, may be expressed in a public situation. Writing about positive memories also allows group members to recognise that they have had happy moments in the past and that they are able to reproduce these for themselves.

4. Writing can help to develop concentration and orientation in time.

In order to facilitate writing, one of the central requirements is that of quietness; the demand is made of group members that they concentrate, and that they do not disturb one another. This in itself helps to encourage an awareness of the need for quiet reflection and of the needs of others. The requirement to write for a concentrated and uninterrupted period of time is central to a sense of seriousness about the work. The time boundaries which are essential to the running of the group also help to facilitate a sense of timekeeping and of what can be achieved within a limited time frame.

5. Writing can promote an awareness of others and of the environment

The practice of writing requires both observation and imagination, and can encourage new perceptions of the immediate surroundings and of the people in the group. The exercises in this book include particular tasks which are designed directly to encourage an observation and appreciation of the group's immediate surroundings, and others which are designed to evoke an imaginative and empathetic response to other people. The experience of the group itself and of sharing written work encourages a mutual respect and new forms of social interaction.

6. Writing can help to develop a sense of self-esteem

The production of a single piece or a collection of writing can promote a sense of pride. If work is kept over the weeks or months of the group members' participation in the group, this can act as an affirmation of the energy and time invested in the group and can serve as an encouragement. This can be very important if a group member becomes particularly self-critical or feels unable to contribute in a session, and acts as a reminder of past achievements. The support and encouragement of other group members is also something which observably reinforces self-esteem.

7. The group is a means of developing writing skills

Although this is not the primary purpose of a creative writing group in a mental health context, the regularity and practice of writing, and the responses of other people to that writing, do mean that group members will develop their skills with language. This has the benefit of increasing confidence, but is also practically useful; writing skills are particularly important for those who are concerned with finding employment. The practice of a writing group can be extended outside the group and, if appropriate, may offer help with the writing of letters and with filling out application forms.

8. The group encourages an appreciation of other forms of writing

Reading is for many people one of life's great pleasures, but for those in a state of crisis, the concentration and patience required for reading a book, or of demanding forms of writing such as poetry, can be hard to find. Poetry, especially, is one of the creative forms most associated with intense and painful feelings, and it can be enormously beneficial for anyone to encounter suggestions of their own experience in a publicly recognised and appreciated form.

The practice of writing and of experimenting with language and with literary forms (see Chapter 11) encourages an understanding and appreciation of different kinds of written work, which can offer participants a way into reading forms of writing which they might otherwise not have attempted, and introduces them to writers that they may not have read before. There are a number of exercises here which borrow from the work of established poets, and which provide a way of engaging the group members with their work.

Requirements for the group

A creative writing group requires very few resources, but it is important to provide a setting that will promote concentration and to supply basic materials. It is most important that the group should meet regularly in the same room, and that this space should be quiet and unobserved so that group members can write and share their work with as little disturbance as possible. A small room with comfortable chairs allows for intimacy, and distances the experience of the writing from that of school. Writing tables or desks are not necessary, as long as members have a hard file or similar surface on which to write, although a small central table can be useful for those exercises which use props, such as postcards or small objects.

Some groups may benefit from the use of prompt cards; this need only be a slip of paper with a clearly written word on it, or a suggestion for a particular theme. Some of the exercises here specify the use of such props (these are clearly indicated in the 'Requirements' section of each exercise); in some groups with members who have impaired memory or concentration skills, the use of a visual or written prompt may prove to be the only way in which the group can begin writing, and these exercises are useful to employ with any group member who has difficulty in getting started with writing.

Pens and paper should be supplied; this signals an institution's commitment to the group, and lends the group's activities the aspect of serious work. A ring binder for each participant is also recommended – these allow members to file their work and to keep it in a safe place. This encourages members to value what they have done, and to recognise after several sessions that they have achieved a substantial body of work which they could develop further. It may be appropriate that the group facilitator(s) collect the files and keep them safe for the next session, although group members should have access to them and should be given the option of keeping them themselves if that is what they prefer. Collecting the work in files allows for an acknowledgement of the work achieved, and makes it easier to go on to develop some public showing of the work in the form of an exhibition or performance if that is what the group chooses.

Group members

Not everyone is suitable for a group of this kind – those who find extreme difficulty in concentrating or who have real language or literacy problems will be frustrated and could be humiliated by the experience of the group. You may need to set up your own guidelines for inclusion in the group in your own working context. However, there are some clear criteria for membership: involvement in the group requires that members are literate, that they are able to concentrate for a reasonable length of time, that they are willing to contemplate sharing their work with the group, that they are able to tolerate a group situation for an entire session, and that they are able to follow and to contribute to group discussion. Potential group members will also need to acknowledge and to abide by the group's rule of confidentiality.

While basic literacy is an important requirement for group members, it is not necessarily those who are obviously articulate or intellectual who will benefit most from the group. An over-facility with words can prove to be inhibiting for both the group and the client, and a self-consciousness or over-literary response to the practice of writing can prove difficult for the group to manage. It is often those who find it most difficult to articulate their emotions who find that creative writing may well be a way into expressing repressed feelings.

Between six and eight members is an ideal number for a group; a small number allows the group to pay proper attention to each person's contribution. Any more and the time required for feedback can become too long. If the group is any smaller, members may feel that too much attention is focused on themselves and their work, and group continuity is difficult to sustain if more than one member is absent in any one week.

It should be stressed at the outset of each group that members join with the understanding that their membership represents a commitment to the group. In order to build up trust and openness within the group, it is important to sustain a familiar environment and the adjustment to new or irregular members of the group disrupts that continuity. For the same reasons, it is advisable that, if possible, no more than two new members should come into the group at any one time.

Literacy

The one requirement of members of the group, apart from confidentiality, is that they should have basic literacy skills and are able to concentrate sufficiently to write for a sustained period of time. If a participant finds it extremely difficult to write, or has great difficulty with written English, it can be that their anxiety will outweigh the benefits that they can gain from the group. New members can often be anxious about grammar and their ability to spell and to punctuate, but it is very important to stress that that is not the purpose of the group. At the beginning of the group, and whenever a new member joins, it should be clearly stated that grammar, punctuation and handwriting are not at all important, but that what matters is that the group member should themselves be able to read their work to the rest of the group. It can also be emphasised that no-one other than themselves will look at the writing, if that is what they choose.

The role of the facilitator

Wallace Stegner, a professor of creative writing in the USA, has described the requirements of a creative writing teacher: 'Negative capability, a phrase that Keats used, is what is needed here: sympathy, empathy, a capacity to enter into another mind without dominating it' (1988, p.44).

Stegner is writing here of an academic tutor's response to student writers, but what he advises is all the more true for those with mental health problems. Sympathy and empathy are vital to any facilitator of a creative writing group. It is a role that requires great resources of sensitivity to others: an awareness of the differences of culture, education, age, class and gender, and an ability to empathise beyond the bounds of one's own experience are essential to each member's trust in the facilitator and to the life of the group.

Once a group is up and running, and its members are familiar with one another and with the formal structures of the group, it may become possible to involve some of the more experienced group members in the planning of a session. Ideas for future sessions may well emerge from evaluation groups and from general discussion. The facilitators can then structure these according to the group's needs.

We would recommend that there are two facilitators in the group. This is partly for practical purposes – if a member of the group has a crisis or leaves the session, then there is someone who can take them away from the group or follow them and someone who can remain and keep the group going. Another reason is that it is important to have another professional person to share the experience of the session and of the group's progress, and to share feedback on the events and individuals of the group. If there are two facilitators, they will each need to clarify their respective roles in a session, and to identify whether their contribution is one of leadership or of support.

The atmosphere of the group should be comfortable, non-threatening, accepting and, most importantly, non-competitive, and it is the most important function of the facilitators that they should promote and ensure that these principles are adhered to in the group. The facilitators' responses to the work at the end of a session are central to this; in providing positive feedback and affirmation of each member's contributions, and in facilitating responses from other members of the groups. The facilitators can develop and support different kinds of imaginative and emotional responses to the exercises and, similarly, are in a position to curtail negative comments on any individual's work, and to encourage an atmosphere of mutual support.

Professional boundaries

It is very important to respect and to bear in mind your own position as a professional facilitator; although the writing process can and should be democratic, it must be remembered that the facilitator's role in the group is different from that of other members. It is strongly recommended (although this ultimately should be left to the judgement of individual facilitators) that all members, including the group leaders, should share their work with the group by reading it aloud. Not to do so is to encourage a distance between group leaders and other members, which does not promote trust. If facilitators do not contribute in the sharing of work this can make other group members feel as if they and their work are being judged. One creative writing facilitator has stressed the importance of the group leaders participating in the sharing of work, in describing his own practice in a hospital writing group:

> I set a writing exercise, which we all do, any staff in the room as well as the patients. This is, in my view, very important. We do not expect the patients to try anything we are not ourselves prepared to try. We do not institute or perpetuate a class system. When everybody is ready... we read back. Discussion follows. (Benson 1987, p.54)

The extent to which the facilitators want to encourage discussion, however, is very much up to them and can be determined by the practices of the institution in which they are working and of the group itself. While feedback and appreciation of the work accomplished is a necessary part of the process, discussion can skate perilously close to interpretation, and this may not be appropriate to the needs of the group.

We would certainly agree that it is important for facilitators to participate in the practice of writing and in sharing their work with the group; but, nonetheless, would recommend that the facilitators are constantly aware of their different relationship to the group and to the process of writing in this context. It is the facilitators' responsibility to set up and maintain the boundaries of the group in a way that is not required of other members. While it might seem undemocratic or hypocritical to expect others to write from personal and distressing experiences and not to share your own, equally it is difficult to pay attention and to respond to other people's work if you are too involved in your own. It is expected of the group facilitator that their role is to monitor the emotions and tensions within the group; it is important to recognise that the experience of writing can take group leaders aback as much as any other member of the group. Your writing may often reveal more about yourself than you would be willing to share with group members in any other professional context.

Writing is always more self-revelatory than the writer can control (see Barthes 1977, pp.142–9 for an account of this concept), and it is wise to set about each writing task with some caution. In order to maintain some professional distance, it is sensible to choose an option that is not too close to a painful or difficult memory, and while writing, to avoid any incident or characters that are too revealing of anything that could be construed as unprofessional. Your own cultural experience or political inclinations may not be in sympathy with those of some other members in the group; in order to sustain the group's trust in you it may be necessary to curb some of your own responses. In some exercises, it might be wise not to be too revealing about your own political or religious affiliations, and so risk alienating some of the group's members.

Problems can also arise if a facilitator is more practised in writing and more fluent than other members of the group. It is necessary for facilitators to restrain any extremes of language or expression in their own work, in order not to intimidate or to constrain writing from other members of the group. This is not a group in which the focus is on the craft of writing; much more it is about facilitating other people to express their emotions in a written form. It is therefore important not to impose a limit or to set up conventions for the 'right' way to write within a group – it is all too easy to establish these unknowingly, and to set up expectations of what the 'proper response' to a task is. The group facilitator has an important function in legitimising different interpretations of the task in hand and in demonstrating that all kinds of different responses are possible and valid.

Approaching the sessions

For many people, the act of writing is in itself an intimidating task to take on, and can all too often be associated with bad memories of essay or composition writing in school – this is particularly true of those who are in an emotionally vulnerable state. There are creative writing groups which have the primary task of developing writing skills and which are there for people who are willing to experiment and to push themselves and their creativity in new and challenging directions. This may well not be the case for those who have been referred to a creative writing group in a psychiatric hospital or similar institution,

Group members are encouraged to produce work on the spot, and time is not given to the checking of the writing; members are encouraged to write an immediate response to the exercise, not to ponder about their work too much, and to explore and to value whatever it is that they produce from the top of their heads. Group members can be advised that if they would like to produce a more polished piece of writing, they can develop and work on a piece of writing outside the group time. Warm-up exercises are a means of introducing a playful and unserious tone to the group, which can often help to release inhibitions and to relax tensions about writing.

The vulnerability of group members and their potential unwillingness to share pain and difficulty within the group needs to be remembered and respected. The exercises here are very tightly structured. This is important in that it encourages every member of the group to write and provides a familiar and secure framework for the expression of difficult and painful feelings. As the group develops, it becomes possible to experiment with different forms of exercise and structures for the session, but in the early stages, it is important to set up a formal framework. Members are invited to respond to the task in whatever way they choose, and to share as much or as little of their work as they are prepared to give to the group.

Group members will often resist any direct demand that they should write about themselves, their feelings or experiences, but if they are asked to write about themselves and their memories in an oblique way, they will often share their experiences very generously and openly. An oblique approach to the task, rather than a requirement to write openly, will often produce revealing insights into a patient's experience of family, current state of being and their perception of their environment. Some of the exercises in this book may initially appear to be banal, but that is precisely why they work – they do not appear to be directly confrontational or to demand that group members share their painful memories. Instead, they appear to be about commonly shared and familiar everyday experiences, and as such they seem unthreatening – they allow participants to interpret them in their own way, and should allow for group members to produce a piece of writing that is bland if that is what they choose to do.

The ordinariness of the experiences and memories demanded by the exercises also allows members to recognise that there may be a range of different responses to the same event. This becomes particularly important when people are asked to write about an occasion that is generally assumed to be positive, such as Christmas, or a holiday. Writing about this in the safe context of the group can allow for negative feelings and memories to emerge, and enable group members to recognise that they are not alone in their unhappy experiences of culturally celebrated festivals and events. A writing group may be one of the few spaces in which it is possible to express such negative feelings.

Writing can be a means of confronting difficult and painful experiences as well as a way of remembering positive memories. Putting these down on paper can be a way of putting such feelings and events into perspective and, in sharing them, recognising that they may not be peculiar to you. It is important to have a sense of how the group develops over the weeks or months of its life, and to allocate exercises accordingly. It can be wearing to have a constantly upbeat tone in the group; not to allocate sessions for the exploration of painful feelings is a means by which the group will repress those feelings. An over-emphasis on one kind of material will skew the group, and not allow the members to develop their own course through their writing.

Confronting group members with a blank piece of paper and asking that they express their feelings can be truly intimidating. Exercises should therefore be carefully structured to ensure that they do not immediately demand revelations – there should always be an escape clause which enables people to hide behind their defences. The most successful work we found to emerge was from work that came at important feelings from an oblique angle, and which did not present itself as particularly revelatory. References to shared cultural experiences; such as folk and fairy tale, children's toys and familiar places offer a means of entry into memories and fantasies that may be very personal, but which need not necessarily be revealed as such to the group. The group member always needs a means of hiding private emotions, if that is what they deem appropriate for themselves at the time.

It may also be the case that there will be group members who are resistant to the structure of the group, and who find this kind of exercise over-directed. The 'Finally' section of each exercise does allow some leeway for adding to the prescribed structure and for members to complete their work in their own way, but this may not be enough for all group members. This may be because they themselves write very fluently, and are frustrated with the limitations of the group, or because they have outlived its usefulness to them. In such cases it may be advisable to refer them to a less formally structured creative writing group and to a more professionally or creatively focused group. (there are suggestions for how to find such groups in Appendix 3). There are other members who may find the process of group cooperation difficult in itself, and who would prefer to do their writing outside the confines of a group; in this case, facilitators can provide a useful support in reading and discussing their work, and perhaps suggesting other contexts in which it might be developed.

You may well find that membership of the group works through self-selection, and that such members may simply not turn up. If you do encounter resistance to the group structure from an individual member, it is important to point out that the function of this particular group is to facilitate writing for everyone, and that many people find the fact that it is directive helpful rather than inhibiting. If there are several group members who express resistance, you may well find that a less structured approach is required.

Ethnic and cultural difference

The cultural and religious affiliations of group members may well not be immediately available to you, but are likely to emerge over the course of the group's life. Religious and cultural beliefs that may be very important to an individual's sense of themselves may not be apparent from case notes or from an initial interview. It is vitally important that group facilitators should not make any assumptions about shared cultural values or identities, and to be sensitive to those ethnic, sexual and religious differences that inevitably will be present among the group. A universality of experience can never be assumed, and it is vital that the sessions are structured in such a way that a marginal or dissident response to the exercise is made possible. This can be achieved by allowing for the options of a positive or negative response to an imagined or actual scenario, and also by constantly acknowledging that not all members of the group will necessarily have the same life experiences.

Exercises organised around a particular religious festival, such as Easter or Christmas, are valid tasks to present to the group because they are so much part of the cultural fabric that they have become unavoidable calendar markers in this country. Nonetheless, such specific tasks should be clearly set up in such a way as to allow for a position of distance to be taken, and it should not be assumed that everyone will mark or celebrate the event.

Be aware of class difference too; it cannot be assumed that what are pleasures to some social groups – such as foreign holidays (or, indeed, holidays at all) or theatre visits – are within everyone's experience. Sexuality cannot be taken for granted either. Do not assume that all members of your group are heterosexual; group members who are gay may well not want their sexuality to be known within the group, but can nonetheless feel excluded if there is an emphasis on exercises about children or family life. Similarly, in work with lesbians and gay men, it cannot be assumed that marriage and children are outside the experience of all those in the group.

Age is another important difference – allow for the fact that certain cultural experiences may not have been available to older group members, and that they may have memories which younger group members will not necessarily recognise. There will be a great range of different personal histories in the group, and the emergence, valuing and sharing of these is among the most valuable things to emerge from the experience of the group.

As trust builds within the group, it may well become possible to incorporate aspects of sexual, class, racial and religious difference into the group's dynamic. At this point, facilitators can begin to devise tasks that explore those different identities in a positive way. This is a development that should, however, be left to the group members to initiate rather than one that is imposed by facilitators.

Literary forms

Any literary form can be adapted into an exercise for a creative writing group. Poetry, prose and drama are all forms which can develop confidence and writing skills and which allow for different kinds of communication and expression. As the group members grow in confidence and in the practice of writing it becomes possible to introduce new and challenging written forms which they may not have tried out before. The last section of exercises in this book, Chapter 11, 'Exploring literary form', introduces poetic forms that could well lead to the reading of other kinds of writing, and help to encourage group members to support their work in the group by the reading of published writers.

Prose

Prose seems to be the simplest and most familiar form of writing, and is therefore a good starting point. Writing prose consistently however can be limited, and does not always stretch group members far enough; it can also come close to negative memories of school essay writing. It is a good idea to offer a variety of different forms of writing: diary entries, letters and reports are familiar and useful modes of writing that can explore the different possibilities and uses of the prose form, and develop group members' skills.

There are exercises in this book which are designed to encourage group members to imagine a character or a setting. At the end of the exercise, it can be pointed out that these pieces of work could be used in a larger project, and offer the basis for a short story or even of a novel. Julia Casterton's book, *Creative Writing: A Practical Guide,* is useful on ways of expanding and developing existing pieces of writing.

As the group develops, it becomes possible to ask group members to combine characters and settings and to set up the beginnings of a narrative. They can be encouraged to develop their ideas in their own time, but it is important that facilitators allow that this will require some form of recognition: this could take the form of allocating time within the group for the reading of work produced outside it, or simply facilitators taking the time to read and to comment on the work.

Poetry

Poetry is a particularly valuable form of writing in a therapeutic context because it offers a means of organising chaotic thoughts into a formal shape and unity. As the literary critic I.A. Richards asserted in the 1920s:

> if there be any means by which we may artificially strengthen our minds' capacity to order themselves, we must avail ourselves of them. And of all possible means, Poetry, the unique linguistic instrument by which our minds have ordered their thoughts, emotions, desires… in the past, seems to be the most serviceable. It may well be a matter of some urgency for us, in the interests of our standards of civilisation, to make this highest form of language more accessible. (1929, p.320)

For those who may be experiencing chaos in their lives, it can be particularly valuable to contain painful and difficult feelings within a very limited generic form. The constraints of the form can act, paradoxically, to require the writer to experiment with language and rhyme, and so free forms of expression which might otherwise not have come to mind.

Many people can, however, feel inhibited at the prospect of writing poetry, and perceive it to be a particularly demanding and difficult form of writing. While poetry is probably best left for a stage in the group when members are developing a confidence in their writing skills, there are a number of exercises that can break down these inhibitions and introduce poetry as a form that members are quite capable of writing. The use of short poetic forms as a warm-up can introduce the group to poetry, and a collective poem is a particularly good way of introducing the group to poetic form in an unintimidating way (in that no one person is implicated in what is produced!). Building up a piece of writing line by line is a means of introducing participants to the idea of rhythm and of poetic language.

Using work by other poets is another means of introducing a range of poetic form and ideas into the group's writing. Borrowing forms or ideas from other poets can introduce people to the poetic voice. Using a line of poetry as a starting point for the group's own poems and then presenting the group with the original is a way of introducing group members to writers they might otherwise not have attempted to read. Any poet or work that works with a very regular form would work very well as the basis of an exercise. Some of these are suggested in Chapter 11, but you may well come across other favourite or suitable poems that could be adapted in similar ways.

Drama

Drama therapy is a discipline distinct from creative writing, and has its own body of theory. Many institutions will have their own drama therapy groups or drama therapists, but nonetheless, dramatic writing is in its very nature about the act of communication, and so has a very useful function to perform in a creative writing group. For those who are in a situation in which it is difficult to feel empathy, it can be enormously beneficial to ask participants to write in the voice of someone else, and a dramatic monologue offers that as a form. As the group members become more familiar with one another, it is possible to ask of them that they write dialogue with each other, and so to begin to write in a range of different voices.

Because drama is a public form, it offers great opportunities for taking the work outside the confines of the group, and for making links with other creative therapy groups. It will take some time, however, for the group to reach the point at which members have the confidence in their skills to share their work with others outside the immediate creative writing group. Experiments with dramatic writing however – even if these never reach the stage of a form that could be produced – are always a form of sharing voices, and this is an important platform which a creative writing group can provide.

Organisation of the group

The rules by which the group is run will depend very much on your client group and their identified needs, on the type of group that you are facilitating and on your institution's policies and procedures. One decision that has to be made before a group begins is the kind of group that it is. Is it a closed group, to which members are referred and to which they make a regular commitment, or an open group which anyone may join for however long they choose? It has been our experience that the mutual trust that is so important to the writing process is best served by a closed group, in which it is clear that the work produced in the group remains confidential and within a limited circle. A closed group also allows facilitators to check that potential members are appropriate to the group, and that the concentration and basic literacy of each member is sufficient for membership to be beneficial to them.

The time scale of each group is also important to consider. Is it a group that runs for a limited period, or an ongoing group which welcomes new members as others leave? A group that runs for a restricted number of weeks may be the best form in which to produce a specific project, but in the context of a hospital, may be difficult to sustain. As members are discharged, but may want to maintain contact with the group, a more open policy might be appropriate.

Introductions

It is useful for a facilitator to have a preliminary interview with each group member before they join the group, both to outline the ground rules of the group and to acknowledge any anxieties that a potential group member may have. This can also serve to address any misplaced expectations that there may be about the potential of the group, and allows the facilitator to explain that the work of the group is directed. At this stage it is important not to probe too deeply into such feelings, and not to pre-empt the member's response to the group. As the group develops and as each member participates in it, different questions and anxieties will emerge, and can be more productively addressed in an evaluation session.

In order to engender a mutual trust within the group, it is very important that all members of the group have a sense of knowing one another and of the rules and framework for the group. It is therefore important to introduce the members when the group first meets, to outline the rules and conventions of the group's organisation, and so to establish a formal beginning. As any new member joins the group, they should be introduced to other members, and the group's regulations should be reiterated.

Rules of the group

The rules of membership of the group should be made clear in any preliminary interview and at the beginning of the first session, and to any new members as they appear. Clearly, the rules will depend on the context of each group, but there are some issues that are common to all groups. Respecting the timing of the group, and allowing members to concentrate are essential features for every creative writing group. Silence during the periods of writing is essential to concentration, and should be a requirement of the group members; facilitators should encourage quiet as the group begins to write. As the group develops, this may no longer be necessary, but occasional reminders are sometimes needed.

In order for trust to be built up and respected within the group, confidentiality is vital, and group members should contract that they will not reveal what has been written outside the group. The exception to this rule is facilitators, who will need to reserve the right to reveal work to other professional colleagues – this should be indicated to the group. In extreme cases, for example, it can happen that writing will indicate suicidal or violent ideas that have not been recognised in other contexts.

Writing can inadvertently reveal feelings and ideas that the writer may not be willing to share – the process of writing involves risk. It is therefore very important that all group members respect the participation and contributions of others, and that they are not judgemental in their own writing or in their responses to other people's writing. This is an approach that facilitators should encourage, and it is, on the whole, the case that the group members are very considerate of each other and of each other's work. In the rare situation that a group member makes unhelpful or critical judgements of another member's writing, facilitators should firmly indicate that this is not the function of this particular group.

There are other practical issues, which will inevitably come up over the course of a group's life, such as whether or not to admit late arrivals to the group, smoking, and the regularity of attendance. Different institutions may have different policies on such issues, but if at all possible, allowing members to vote on these concerns does enable them to have a sense of owning their own group and of being involved in decisions.

Structure of the session

Each session will usually consist of a short warm-up exercise, followed by a related longer task. This isn't a set pattern and, as the group develops, it can be varied according to its needs. It is advisable at the beginning of a group's life, however, to establish a formal pattern of working, and the short exercise does allow for a flexing of the imagination and of language skills before a longer task is undertaken. As a group becomes more confident with writing and with each other it becomes possible to move straight into a longer writing exercise, or to develop work from one session into another. It may take some time until the group is ready to depart from a familiar framework, however.

Sharing work

The sharing of work is an integral part of the group process, in that it allows for an appreciation of the work achieved and creates a formal ending for each group session. It also enables group participants to recognise that they may not be alone in their responses to a task. One of the essential functions of the facilitator is to keep the time of the group within bounds, and it is most important that the sharing of work is considered within that timing. Ensure that there is sufficient time for each member to read out the work that they have produced in each session, and for other members to have proper time to respond. In a group where each member is writing with concentration, facilitators can find it hard to interrupt and to stipulate that writing time is over, but the sharing of work is of vital importance and it is crucial not to bite into the time allowed for this.

As Stegner has said of creative writing students:

Merely having a story read aloud and discussed makes it, in its author's eyes, more serious and worthy. And that group around the table may be the best audience, though not the biggest, that that writer will have in his life. (1988, p.63)

For many with mental health problems, to have an audience for their work at all can be a new and validating experience, and to have their work listened to with seriousness can help to engender feelings of worthiness that extends beyond the written work. There may be occasions on which any group member would prefer not to share their writing with the group, and that choice should be respected as valid.

There are differing opinions as to the extent to which the facilitators should comment on and interpret the work. This will, up to a point, depend on your own practice and experience and on the dynamics within the group. However, it is important to remember that the function of the group is not to improve or to publicly scrutinise members' writing. There are other creative writing groups in which that is the primary purpose, and if a group member particularly wants comments and advice on their writing, it may be the time to direct them to a local creative writing group.

There will be also be times when it is very tempting to interpret a group member's written work, if they have revealed themselves in ways of which they are unaware, or if their writing throws up insights into their diagnosis or condition. But it is important to be careful and very sparing with interpretations – they may well not be welcomed and can distract from the primary purpose of the group, which is to encourage writing. If creative writing is understood as a form of occupational therapy, in which the participants can leave the group with something that they have created and of which they can be proud, then it may not be appropriate to comment upon the work and to perhaps diminish it for its writer.

The reading back of work is an opportunity for the facilitator to give positive feedback and to encourage people to continue with their writing. There may be a great disparity in the abilities of the group members, but it is important to encourage everyone equally, and to find connections between the contributions. If a member has struggled to put something onto paper, then that is as worthy of encouragement and approval as is an elegant and imaginative piece of writing.

The discussion of the work at the end of each session should focus on similarities and differences in responses to the task rather than interpretations of individual pieces, and allows facilitators to bring the themes of the session together and to formally close it.

Evaluation

Once the group has established a sense of familiarity and of cohesion, it is important to allow space for the group and its members to take stock of the experience of the group, to explore the benefits of membership, and to acknowledge any difficulties that have been encountered. This evaluation should not detract from the creative process and from the group dynamic, but rather enhance these, in that it enables an open dialogue between facilitators and other group members. Clearly, the way in which evaluation is approached will depend on the client group and on the kind of group that you are running; whatever the context, some form of evaluation which involves all the group members allows for individual members' experience of the group to be articulated and valued. It is also important that the facilitators should assess their own performances, and an evaluation session is a useful way of monitoring the group's development.

It is important to give the group prior warning that an evaluation session is programmed, in order to give the individual members time to consider if they have any unmet needs or expectations for the future of the group. An evaluation session should only take place when every member of the group has had the experience of at least several weeks' participation, and has built up a body of work.

Each group will have their own set of ongoing concerns and criticisms and comments from members, but there are a number of ways in which a structured evaluation session can be set up, and which can help to incorporate and address these issues, as shown in the following examples.

1.   Ask each member to look through their file of work and to choose their favourite piece of writing. This is then read out to the group, and the group member explains why this was the one that they chose. This process can be used for the entire session, and works to validate the writing, but it can also be useful as a warm-up activity to initiate a more rigorous evaluation discussion.

2.   Each member is asked to write down their own understanding of the purpose of the group on a slip of paper. These are then placed in the centre of the group and members take turns to pick a slip, and then to discuss what is written. It should be emphasised at the beginning of this activity that while each person's view point is valid, judgements or criticisms of other people's contributions (or work) are not permissible. All the written points should be brought into the evaluation, by the facilitators if necessary – even a blank piece of paper merits some discussion!

3. The facilitators prepare slips of paper on which are written some of the potential benefits and limitations of the group. These can provide the basis for discussion, or members can be invited to use the points which they find relevant to them to write about their own experience of the group. This may be more appropriate if there are group members who need more prompting than Activity 2 above provides.

4. Ask group members to write down suggestions for future group sessions, and for ways in which they would like the group or their own work to proceed. This provides a space for group members to express their ambitions for their writing, and for the group to support this and advise them on how to progress. This support can be practically confirmed if facilitators come prepared with a list of useful books and groups, and with ideas on how group members can develop their work outside the group.

The evaluation process can be used to generate ideas about the group itself, and can provide insights into issues and themes that the group would like to address in future work. It also provides an opportunity for establishing ways in which the group's work could be made accessible outside the group, and is a good point at which to suggest an exhibition, performance or other form of public display. It is important that the group's comments and criticisms are properly acknowledged and taken on board by facilitators, and good reasons given for why some suggestions cannot be implemented, if that be the case.

Beyond the group

There is great potential for taking the work that the group has achieved outside the group, if the group members themselves are agreeable and enthusiastic about a public showing of their writing. One simple way of organising this is to organise a reading, perhaps to other members of the institution. This could further be developed into performance, particularly if there is opportunity for collaboration with other departments.

Another idea would be to produce a collection of published work which, with the increased availability of word processors, is now possible for most institutions. Some organisations may have access to printing and production facilities, in which case the production of a book could become a long-term project for the group.

Clearly, the possibilities will depend on the length and commitment of your own group, and the facilities available to you. However, the public display, in performance or printed form, of their own work can offer group members a means of articulating their ideas in a public forum, and promote a great sense of satisfaction. Many group members can under-estimate their own work, and a public airing of it can give it a validation that the group itself may not.

Conclusion

Writing is a form of creativity that allows people to play safely with different possibilities. As Freud (1908, p.63) points out:

> The child's best-loved and most intense occupation is with his play or games. Might we not say that every child at play behaves like a creative writer, in that he creates a world of his own, or rather, rearranges the things of his world in a new way which pleases him?

Those undergoing the experience of mental distress, for whatever reason, are in a situation that requires of them that they have to recreate their world in a new way with which they can live. Writing allows for the exploration of different possibilities of organisation, for new modes of self-presentation, for articulating extremes of emotion. But it is a safe way of exploring what it is to assume different identities and modes of expression, and because it is written down, it is put into a public form, and the writer can easily disown it as a work of imagination, and safely distance themselves.

Freud has described the practice of creative writing as the expression of phantasies. Here, Freud 's term 'phantasies' (see Laplanche and Pontalis (1988) for an account of this concept) refers to unconscious wishes that are distorted by defence processes; as he points out:

> We may lay it down that a happy person never phantasises, only an unsatisfied one. The motive forces of phantasies are unsatisfied wishes, and every single phantasy is the fulfilment of a wish, a correction of unsatisfying reality. (1908, p.134)

For people in a state of distress, the need to correct 'unsatisfying' reality is urgent. A creative writing group is a safe place in which to articulate repressed wishes and in which to produce phantasies in a constructive rather than a destructive form. In Freud's terms, if fantasies become 'over-luxuriant and over-powerful', then they are potentially damaging. One of the means by which such fantasies do become over-powerful is if they find no form of expression outside the individual. Sharing them can diminish their power.

When Wallace Stegner was asked what it was that students of creative writing most needed, his answer was:

> They need to be taken seriously. They need to be assured that their urge to write is legitimate. And, even when they must be discouraged from wasting their lives in a hopeless effort, they must not be dismissed flippantly – these are hearts you are treading on. Before a teacher tells anyone he is good, he had better make sure of what he is saying; before he discourages anyone, he had better remember how intimate a thing writing is and how raw the nerves that surround it. (1988, p.25)

A creative writing group facilitator is not a teacher, nor are the members of the group students as such, but this remains excellent advice. The raw nerves surrounding the experience of writing are extra-charged for those with mental health problems.

CHAPTER 2

Warm-Up Exercises

The warm-up exercise is an integral part of each session. It functions to provide a bridge between the writing group and the world outside it, and to mark the group process as a distinct activity. It also helps to introduce the quiet and concentration necessary for writing, and allows group members to become familiar with the practice of writing and the sharing of their work in a group.

Warm-ups are also important because they get people writing, and because they are short, they are relatively unthreatening. The warm-up exercise is playful and should not be taken too seriously; group members are invited to respond spontaneously, and it should not last longer than ten minutes. The object of the warm-up exercise is to get people writing, and to write without correcting or reading through their work. Each exercise should be very accessible, and should be carefully directed so that it is as simple as possible, with very clear instructions. It is helpful, but not essential, that the warm-up exercise relates in some ways to the main task: these exercises very much set the tone for the main writing task, and it is possible to direct the group towards a particular theme or tone of writing through the choice of warm-up.

Each of the writing exercises has a recommended warm-up attached to it, but there is no rule that this is the most appropriate for your group at that particular session. You may well find that there are others which would work better for a particular exercise, or prefer to develop your own.

There are three simple structures for devising a warm-up exercise:

1. A list of three or five positive and/or negative points about a particular theme that is to be developed in the main exercise.

2.   Asking the group to describe a favourite – or least favourite (or both) – place/memory/object that is appropriate to the theme of the session.

3.   A list of between six to ten words (depending on the group) that each group member associates with the theme of the session.

These exercises should last only for five to ten minutes, in order to allow group members to write a short piece, or even a set of words, without worrying about it too much. Many of these exercises are based on word games and provide a means of breaking down inhibitions about writing. Asking members to read out these short pieces also helps to familiarise the group with the sharing of their writing, and a positive response to this introductory work can help to create an environment that supports the main writing task.

Introductions

The following warm-up exercises are largely for use in the early stages of the group, and are often good ways of introducing the group members to one another, and of familiarising the group and the facilitators with each others' names.

○ **Name game**

Take the first letter of your first name and the first letter of your last name (e.g. DP). You can use a middle name as well if you choose.

First, write your name as the first line, including your middle name if you are using it.

Now, take the letters from your name, and use them to write words or a phrase that has something to do with you (e.g. Definitely Peculiar).

Do the same thing again.

And again.

Now finish by using your name as a last line.

Notes: This is particularly useful for a first session, as it helps group members to identify one another, and helps the group facilitators to remember names. It is also a good and unthreatening means of introducing people, in that this is a playful and relatively simple task. The exercise need not be restricted to five lines, but could be expanded to any length.

○ **I am and I like**

Write one sentence that begins 'I am' and that describes something about who you are.

Now write one sentence that begins 'I like' and that describes something that you like very much (this need have no relation to the first sentence).

Now write four lines that use all the words you have used in any order that you like.

Now repeat the first two lines: 'I am' and 'I like'.

Notes: This is based on a poem by Wendy Cope: 'The Uncertainty of the Poet' (Cope 1988). It may be appropriate to have copies of the poem to hand, in order to demonstrate that this kind of play with words does have a respectable poetic lineage! Again, there is no need to restrict the length of the poem, and it is possible to allow people to extend the structure for as long as they wish.

Opening up

These are exercises that are more self-revealing, and are appropriate when you have reached a point at which members feel comfortable and familiar with one another and the group.

○ **True or false?**

Write down three facts about yourself that are true, and one that is not true.

Now swap with the person to your left, and see if you can both identify the untrue fact in each others' lists.

Notes: This is a good way of getting the group to know one another better, and can reveal some surprising information about its members.

○ **Surprises**

Write down one thing about yourself that people who know you would find surprising.

Notes: This warm-up can challenge the image that group members present to the world, and is therefore a useful warm-up to use at the point at which the group is beginning the 'Opening up' section of exercises (Chapter 9).

○ **Special knowledge**

Think about something of which you have a special knowledge or expertise. This could be a job that you've done, a skill, a hobby, or a subject you know about or a special way of doing something – it could be knitting, weight training, cooking or a book that you've read. Explain what it is, and how it is that you come to know about it.

○ **Me**

Write down five things that you like about yourself and five things that you dislike. It must be an equal number.

Notes: Many people will find it easier to write about five things they dislike about themselves, so it is important to stress that they must come up with an equal number of positive things.

○ **I'd like to be**

Write the name of a person that you would like to be for a day (anyone outside the group) and explain why they are the person you chose to write about.

○ **Words**

Invent a word that describes the way that you are feeling today. Write a dictionary definition of your word, and then write a sentence using that word.

General themes

These are warm-up exercises that are appropriate to any exercise, and which can be slotted in to mark a particular event or to fit in at any time of the year.

○ **Media**

Describe a film, book or television programme that has made an impression on you, and explain why that is the one that you chose to write about.

Notes: This is a good way of introducing cultural experiences outside the group, and could be applied to music, paintings or any art form appropriate to the theme of the session. If you want to direct the session even further, it would be possible to specify the genre of film or fiction (e.g. horror, romance, thriller).

○ **Seasons**

Write down seven things that you associate with this time of the year.

Notes: This is a useful way to introduce poetic writing, in that these seven points can be used in the body of the main task. It is appropriate to many other exercises as well, and can be used at any time of the year.

○ **Object**

Write about an object that you treasure and explain why that is.

○ **Saved**

In a fire you are allowed to retrieve one thing. This includes animals, plants and people. What would it be and why?

Notes: This exercise allows group members to talk about something that is of great value to them, and so to learn more about one another.

○ **Names**

Provide a number of names (remember to include a range that acknowledges the ethnic mix of your group, but choose names that do not belong to any member of the group) on slips of paper. Ask each group member to select one, and to write about the associations that that name conjures up for them. What sort of person has this name? What does it suggest to you? Does this name have any particular associations? It could be a relative, a friend, someone famous, or even the name of somebody you hardly know such as the newsagent.

Exploring literary form

○ **Found poem**

Have ready a range of short written texts, such as newspaper and magazine extracts. Ask each group member to choose five sentences from these texts, and to arrange them in whichever order they choose.

○ **Group poem**

Ask each member of the group to write a sentence and to give a copy to every member. Every group member writes a poem, using as many of the sentences they have been given as they can, and in whichever order they wish.

These suggestions will give you the basis from which to develop your own warm-up exercises. It is possible to construct an entire session around warm-up exercises, and this may well be appropriate at the beginning of a group. Many of the exercises are about playing with words, and these word games can be a good way of limbering up in the early stages of a group. It can be that responses to the warm-up prove to be more revealing and interesting than the writing of a longer task.

CHAPTER 3

Beginnings

These are exercises which are particularly suitable for use in the early stages of a group's formation; they are designed to facilitate writing at a point at which many members may feel insecure, and also to introduce the members of the group to one another. They also establish the structure of the group – a regular format to the organisation of the work will help to familiarise group members with the practice of writing and help to make it less intimidating. This structure can be departed from once the group is up and running, its members are comfortable with one another and with the group itself, and more confident in their own writing. These are also exercises which are a useful point to return to when new members come into the group.

The exercises which involve group participation should be left to a later stage in the group's development, as the interaction and cooperation involved may prove challenging to group members who have anxieties about writing in itself. The early exercises in this section are a means of introducing the basic principles of writing and of establishing the formal elements of producing a piece of prose. The first three exercises here are designed so that each group member will have produced a character, setting and the beginnings of a narrative. Because the first two rely on visual prompts, they are a relatively easy way for group members to begin writing.

◦ **Portraits**

Requirements: A sufficient number of postcards of portraits for each member of the group and the facilitators, and a couple extra to allow choice. Be aware of the gender, age and race balance of the group and select the portraits accordingly. This exercise works best if the portraits are not immediately recognisable, and the group are not aware of the subjects' identity.

Recommended warm-up: What is your favourite picture or photograph of a person and why?

Structure: Look very closely at your postcard for a few minutes.

1. Describe what you see in the picture.

2. What is the person wearing, and why did they choose those clothes?

3. Who is this person, and what do they do? You might like to give them a name.

4. Where do they live? Do they live alone, or with other people?

5. How do they feel at the moment this picture was taken/painted?

Finally: Take one last look to check if there are any details that you have not included.

Notes: This is a particularly good exercise for use at the beginning of a group; the postcard acts as a prompt to give group members a starting point that facilitates writing and imagination. It is helpful to note to group members that what they have written is a work of their own imagination, and that the picture only worked as a starting point from which they themselves developed a character. This exercise can usefully be followed up by the 'Landscape' exercise – the two together demonstrate that group members are capable of developing both fictional characters and settings, which can be extended into a longer piece of writing.

○ **Landscape**

Requirements: A sufficient number of postcards of landscapes for each member of the group and the facilitators, and a couple extra to allow choice. The landscapes should include a range of different rural and city scenes, and should preferably be unfamiliar places, unknown to members of the group.

Recommended warm-up: Describe a landscape that has been important to you.

Structure: Look very closely at your postcard for a few minutes.

1. Where are you in this scene? And what are you doing?

2. Describe the environment you are in.

3. What sounds can you hear?

4. Are you aware of any particular smells?

5. How does it feel to be in this place?

Finally: Take one last look to check if there are any details that you have not included.

Notes: This is a very good follow up to the 'Portraits' exercise, and again works well for the first sessions of the group, in that the props of the postcards work to encourage writing and to stimulate imagination. As in the above exercise, it can be pointed out to the group that in these two exercises they have created both a character and a setting, and that these could be developed further into a short story, or even go on to form the basis of a novel.

○ Consequences

Requirements: None.

Recommended warm-up: Play a quick game of consequences. The names could either be real people, or imaginary. It would be wise to stipulate that the names should not be those personally known to the group, although the names of famous people can be used. A brief reminder of the game's structure:

> x meets y
> at x place
> at x time
> x said to y
> y said to x
> and the consequence was...

Structure: Using the structure of the game, now write a longer version, using imaginary people.

1. Invent a male character, give him a name and briefly describe him. Pass the paper to the person on your left.

2. Invent a female character, give her a name and briefly describe her. Pass the paper on.

3. Where do they meet? Describe a real or imaginary place. Pass the paper on.

4. At what time, and at what time of year did they meet? Pass the paper on.

5. Describe his reaction to her and what he said to her. Pass the paper on.

6. What was her reaction to him, and what did she reply? Pass the paper on.

7. What happens next? Pass the paper on.

Finally: Read through the story that you have so far, and add anything that you think it needs to bring it to an end and that makes sense of the story.

Notes: This is a playful way of introducing the group to story telling, and to the basic principles of narrative. As a collective exercise, it is not threatening, as every member of the group is implicated in the final versions of the stories.

○ **Fruit**

Requirements: None.

Recommended warm-up: What is your favourite kind of fruit, and why?

Structure: You are standing in front of a bowl of fruit.

1. Describe the bowl with the fruit in it.

2. The bowl is in a space – where is it placed?

3. Describe the room, the light and the colours.

4. Someone comes into the room and takes one of the pieces of fruit. Describe this person and their action.

5. What happens next?

Finally: Is there anything else that you would like to add? Or, how might you develop from this beginning?

Notes: This is a more serious but still relatively simple way of introducing the group to the writing of narrative, and is a good progression from the invention of a character and setting in the 'Portrait' and 'Landscape' exercises above.

○ **Story wheel**

Requirements: A sheet of paper for each member of the group with the first sentence of a story written at the top. Examples of sentences which suggest a narrative to follow are:

• One day I was thinking…

• It was an empty street, but then…

• That day I made a decision…

Recommended warm-up: Each group member writes the first two words of a sentence, and then passes the paper to their neighbour, who adds another one or two words. The paper is circulated until each sheet has been round each member of the group, and the sentence is completed.

Structure: Take one of the sentences, and think about how it might be developed into a story.

1. Write a few lines to create the beginning of the story.

2. Pass the paper to the person on your left, and continue with the next stage of the story.

3. Pass the paper to the person on your left, and build on what the writers before you have given you.

4. Pass the paper on, and continue to build on the story as it is so far.

5. Continue this until the paper has arrived back with the person who began the story.

6. Bring the story to a conclusion.

Finally: Add anything extra that you feel the story might need to end it. Read out the whole story.

Notes: This is a good means of introducing the writing of narrative in a way that does not implicate any one writer. It is also a very useful exercise in cooperation, and therefore appropriate to the early stages of a group. The stages of development in the story will depend on the number of people in your group, and can be expanded or contracted accordingly.

○ **Colours**

Requirements: The names of colours – e.g. Red, Blue, Yellow, Green, Purple, Orange – written on a sheet of paper in large letters and preferably in the appropriate colours, which is placed in the centre of the room at the point of introducing the main task.

Recommended warm-up: What is your favourite colour, and why?

Structure: Take each of these colours in turn, and write about the associations, feelings and memories that each colour sparks off for you. This could take the form of a list.

1. Red

2. Blue

3. Yellow

4. Green

5. Purple

Finally: Write your lists into a form that has some kind of structure. This could be a poem or a short piece of prose. Use the work that you have already, and then add a finishing line.

Notes: These lists could easily be expanded into a poem, if the exercise has been introduced at a point in the group at which members feel some confidence in their writing ability. This is a good way of introducing the group to the implications and associations of particular words, and is a gentle means of beginning a more imaginative and allusive style of writing.

○ **Object**

Requirements: An exotic object, such as a crystal, stone, or any other similar decorative object, that has no identifiable function and which is not identifiable as belonging to the facilitators or to any other group member. Put the item in the centre of the group.

Recommended warm-up: What is the strangest object that you have ever seen? Describe it briefly, and explain why it was so strange.

Structure: Look at this object for a few minutes.

1. Describe this object.

2. Pick it up and examine it closely. How does it feel to touch?

3. Where do you think it came from? Describe the environment.

4. Does it have a function? What is it used for?

5. Who owns this object, and how did they come by it?

Finally: Is there anything else that you would like to add about this object?

Notes: This exercise can employ any kind of exotic object, the more obscure the better. We have had success with a sandstone desert rose. As the group develops, it would be possible to ask group members to bring objects of their own to act as the basis of a piece of writing. The exercise could also be developed by bringing in a group of objects, or asking each member to bring in an object, and to use the stages of the exercise to link them together in a story.

○ **Collective fairy tale**

Requirements: At least two blank sheets of paper for each group member.

Recommended warm-up: What is your favourite fairy tale, and why?

Structure: Begin by writing 'Once upon a time...'

1. Begin by describing the setting for your fairy tale, is it a castle? A forest? Now pass the paper to the person next to you.

2. Read through what you have been given, and now introduce a heroine into that setting. Pass the paper on.

3. Read through what you have been given, and go on to introduce a hero into the story. Pass the paper on.

4. Read through what you have been given, and introduce something that threatens the hero or heroine. Pass the paper on.

5. Introduce a magical object that deals with the threat. Pass the paper on.

Finally: Read through the completed fairy tale. Is there anything else that you need to add? Then write: 'And they all lived happily ever after...'

Notes: This is a very good exercise for breaking down inhibitions about writing, in that everyone is implicated in the piece of work produced, but no single contribution can be identified as that of one individual. It is also a playful exercise which can produce a measure of hilarity – a good thing at the beginning of the group in that it demonstrates that writing and group work can be fun.

This exercise is a variation on and very simplified version of Vladimir Propp's analysis of the folk tale, in which he claims that all folk tales are made up of 31 fixed elements (see Eagleton 1996 for a brief account of Propp's theory of narratology). Clearly, not all of Propp's elements can be covered in the time allocated to most groups; nonetheless, Propp's model does indicate ways in which this exercise could be expanded: animals, witches, helpers are among the 'actants' he cites that could be introduced into the stages of the task. It might well be appropriate to tell the group of Propp's model at the end of the exercise, in order to quell any suggestion that the writing of fairy tales is a childish and trivial activity.

CHAPTER 4

Introductory Work

These are exercises which require more self-revelation, and which introduce the members to some of the routines and concerns of each others' daily lives. They will help to break down any inhibitions about writing, and also to build an atmosphere of mutual trust within the group. These exercises can help to work as ice-breakers, and serve to introduce the tastes and interests of the members of the group to one another. They also encourage group members to write about things that are important to them and to introduce some of the details of their lives. This section can offer a good transition into the 'Opening up' section of exercises, in that they do ask the group to reveal aspects of their private lives, although in a less direct and personal way. These exercises also allow members to acknowledge shared and different experiences, and to begin to explore their attitudes towards the group.

○ **Getting to the group**

Requirements: None.

Recommended warm-up: What is your favourite way of travelling, and why?

Structure: Think about your journey to the group today.

1. Where do you begin from? Describe the place that you leave behind.

2. What preparation do you make before setting off, and what checks do you make?

3. How do you travel? Describe the walk to the bus or train, or the route that you take if you walk.

4. Describe the journey, and the environment that you move through.

5. Was there anything special that you noticed on your journey?

Finally: What thoughts are going through your mind as you make your way here, and how does it feel to arrive?

Notes: This is an exercise that could be turned into a piece of fictional writing, by asking the group to turn their writing into a third person account of the same events. It is clearly not an exercise which can be used if some or all of your group are in-patients.

○ **Clothes**

Requirements: None.

Recommended warm-up: What is your favourite item of clothing, and what is it about it that makes it your favourite?

Structure: Think about what you are wearing today.

1. Where did at least three of the items come from?

2. Do any of them have particular associations or memories?

3. Why did you choose to put these items on today?

4. Is there anything about your clothes that gives particular clues about the kind of person you are?

5. What do you think your clothes say about you? How do you want people to see you?

Finally: Is there anything else that you would like to say about your clothes and what you think that they reveal about you?

Notes: This can be a very revealing exercise, and is useful in the early stages of the group, because it can often help to break down assumptions that group members may have about one other. It is, however, quite demanding to ask members to examine their self-presentation, and so should be kept until there is a good degree of trust and confidence in the group. This also works as a useful means of bringing in group members who may have found it difficult to contribute to the group, particularly those who clearly care about their appearance.

○ **Favourite things**

Requirements: None.

Recommended warm-up: What is the best present that you have ever received, and what was it that made it special?

Structure: Think of your favourite object in your possession at the moment.

1. What is this object? Does it have a function, or is it purely decorative?

2. Describe this object in more detail, including its shape, colour, how it feels to touch, and any distinctive features that it may have.

3. Where is it from, and how do you come to have this object?

4. Where do you keep this object? Why do you keep it in that place?

5. Do you share this object with anyone, do you show it to people, or do you keep it to yourself?

Finally: What is it about this object that makes it particularly special to you?

Notes: This is an exercise that could be used as a transition from introductory work into work that is more revealing, but it is still appropriate to the early stages of a group in that writing about an object does not initially appear to be too personal. For those who have been in an institution for some time it may be difficult to identify a particular object, so it is important to stress that the object might be an item of clothing, a photograph or letter.

○ **Animals**

Requirements: None.

Recommended warm-up: Write down one kind of animal that you particularly like, and one that you particularly dislike, explaining why this is.

Structure: Think of an animal you've known and feel strongly about, either because you are or have been very fond of it, or because you dislike or disliked it intensely.

1. Describe this animal.

2. What is its name? How did it come by this name?

3. How did this animal come to be a part of your life?

4. What is it about this animal that you particularly like or dislike?

5. Why is this the animal that you remember particularly and have chosen to write about?

Finally: Is there anything more that you feel you would like to say about this animal?

Notes: For most people, animals evoke positive feelings. But it is important to remember that some people can have phobic reactions to animals, or have distressing memories of the loss of an animal that was close to them. Be prepared for these kind of responses, include the option of writing about the dislike of an animal, and acknowledge the extent of dislike if it should emerge in the reading of work. This exercise could also form the basis of a poem.

○ **A day out**

Requirements: None.

Recommended warm-up: Write down five things that you associate with spring/summer/autumn/winter. (According to the season, you could choose to concentrate on one, or include all of these.)

Structure: Think of a special day out or a day on holiday – choose any day that is not typical of your life.

1. Where are you? Describe the setting.

2. What is the weather like? How does it make you feel?

3. What can you see?

4. Is anyone with you? Describe being with them, or describe how it feels to be by yourself.

5. Does anything happen?

Finally: What was it that made that day particularly memorable?

Notes: It is important not to assume that all group members will have experienced holidays, and it is therefore important that the facilitators do not write about anything that is too enviably exotic.

CHAPTER 5

Memories

Positive memories

These exercises are designed to evoke happy memories from the past, and to promote the recognition of pleasures. The memories are useful in promoting a recognition of shared experience, and also in allowing group members to get to know one another and to get a sense of other people's histories. It is important, however, to recognise that the loss of important people or places may bring up very painful feelings, and that there can be very ambivalent responses to these memories. It cannot be assumed that all the members of the group will react positively to the exercises, and it is important to allow for these responses and to acknowledge them in discussion. Some of the themes of the exercises here will not provoke happy memories for all the members of the group; these are signalled in the notes, but there may be cases in your own group which we cannot anticipate – facilitators should be prepared for negative responses to any one of these exercises.

These exercises are nonetheless appropriate for particularly difficult points in the group's life. If one or more members is depressed, it can be useful to remind the group of times in the past at which they have experienced pleasure. These should not, however, be over-used and should be interspersed with other kinds of exercise. Group members will resist any expectation that all sessions should be upbeat and positive, and it is vitally important that the group is seen as a place which allows space for negative feelings and memories, and which does not necessarily require its members to be positive.

○ **Relaxation**

Requirements: None.

Recommended warm-up: Write down three things that make you tense, and then three things that you find relaxing.

Structure: Think of a place in which you have felt very relaxed; this could be out of doors or indoors. Shut your eyes for a moment, and imagine yourself in this place.

1. How do you physically feel in this place?

2. Stretch out an arm – what can you feel around you? (Your eyes are still shut.)

3. What sounds are you aware of?

4. Open your eyes. What can you see immediately?

5. Look around you – describe where you are.

Finally: Is there anything else that you would like to add about this place and the feeling of being there?

Notes: This is a variation on a relaxation exercise but it does not specify the kind of place that should be imagined. It can be beneficial for group members to have the experience of feeling relaxed committed to paper, and for them to recognise that this is a feeling that they can evoke for themselves.

○ **Journey**

Requirements: None.

Recommended warm-up: Describe one place of which you have very happy memories (not somewhere that you live or have lived) and would like to return to, and one place which you've visited that you never want to revisit.

Structure: Think of a special trip that you have taken in the past.

1. Where did you travel from? By what means of transport?

2. How did you travel – alone or with company?

3. What were the travelling conditions like, both inside and outside your means of transport?

4. What can you see out of the window as the journey unfolds?

5. Where do you arrive and what is the first thing that you do there? What are your impressions when you first arrive?

Finally: Why was that trip particularly special for you?

Notes: The emphasis on the journey rather than the arrival in this exercise means that it is often interpreted as a metaphorical rather than a literal journey. Whatever journey is chosen, it will often be one that is associated with a significant life event. It is possible to direct this exercise towards memories of childhood holidays by including the question 'How old were you?' at the beginning.

○ **Games**

Requirements: None.

Recommended warm-up: Describe one game that you really enjoy, and one that you really dislike, and explain why.

Structure: Think of a game that you really enjoyed playing as a child. It can be a board game, indoor or outdoor game, but should be one that you played often.

1. Describe this game, and how you played it.

2. Did you need any equipment to play the game? Describe what you used.

3. Where did you play this game?

4. Did you play this game by yourself, or with other people? Who were they?

5. Have you played this game since? What were the circumstances?

Finally: Why was that the game you chose to write about, and what was it about it that you enjoyed?

Notes: It cannot be assumed that all group members had childhood friends, and you may well find that people will write about games that they played alone. It is therefore important to include the option of playing a game alone, and to be prepared for memories of being lonely. Again, facilitators should take care not to describe a game that may be beyond the experience of the group.

○ **Favourite places**

Requirements: None.

Recommended warm-up: Describe a place that you are particularly fond of and that was important to you in the past.

Structure: Think of your favourite place: a town, village, or general area, somewhere that has been important to you in the past, or that is important in the present.

1. Describe this place.

2. What kind of landscape is this place in?

3. What kind of weather do you associate with this place?

4. Are there any buildings that you should describe?

5. Are there any important people that you associate with this place?

Finally: What is it about this place that makes it your favourite?

Notes: Again, this may well bring up childhood memories. It is important to recognise that happy memories may well bring up feelings of loss, and to be prepared for melancholy responses to the exercise. Giving the group the option of writing about significant places either in the past or in the present allows the members to choose how they want to respond to the exercise, and how much of their past they want to reveal.

○ **Perfect day**

Requirements: None (although the session could benefit from having copies available of Rupert Brooke's poem 'Day That I Have Loved' (Rogers 1987)).

Recommended warm-up: Write down your favourite place, your favourite kind of music, your favourite company, your favourite food and your favourite drink.

Structure: You are planning your perfect day, which can incorporate some or all of the above.

1. Where are you? Describe the environment.

2. What can you hear?

3. Is anyone with you?

4. What would you like to eat and drink?

5. How does the day end?

Finally: Is there anything else about the day that made it special?

Notes: This is a good exercise for use at the beginnings of a group, as it is a means of introducing people's tastes to one another. A section of Rupert Brooke's 'Day That I

Have Loved' offers a model for how this exercise might be extended and turned into a poem, and it might be useful to have copies of this to hand.

○ **Cats/dogs**

Requirements: None.

Recommended warm-up: What is your favourite kind of animal, and why?

Structure: Think of a cat or a dog, either one that you know or have known personally, or an imaginary animal.

1. Describe how this cat/dog moves.

2. How does its coat feel?

3. Describe this cat's/dog's face.

4. What sounds does it make?

5. How would you describe this cat's/dog's character, and how does it behave with human beings?

Finally: Structure what you have written into a piece of prose or a poem, incorporating all the points you have made above. It can be about a particular animal, or the species in general.

Notes: This is similar to the 'Animals' exercise in the previous chapter, but more directly allows the group members to write about a pet or animal that has been important to them personally. Again, the option of disliking the species of cats and dogs should be allowed for. It is not essential to include the final section, and to allow the group to read what they have written before the last stage, but this is an exercise in which it is possible to encourage the group to develop from the five-point structure of writing exercises into new and different forms of writing.

Evoking the past

These are exercises designed to allow group members to describe and share aspects of their childhoods and of more recent past histories. They offer an oblique way into autobiography, without directly asking group members to write about childhood memories. It is important to acknowledge that some of these memories may be very painful, and to allow members a measure of choice in approaching the theme of the session. Facilitators should take care not to elicit more than the group members are prepared to share, and to allow for this by presenting the exercises and responding to the work in such a way that different kinds of responses are validated.

○ Cinema

Requirements: The names of a range of well-known films on slips of paper, enough for each member of the group and the facilitators, and a couple extra to allow a choice. Suggestions might include *Casablanca, Mary Poppins, Bambi, Cinderella, Brief Encounter, Star Wars, Alien, Beauty and the Beast* and *Singing in the Rain,* but use your knowledge of your own group to ensure that the titles will be familiar to everyone.

Recommended warm-up: Who is your favourite film star or celebrity? Describe what it is that you like about them.

Structure: Choose one of these films that you have seen.

1. Where did you see this film?

2. How old were you?

3. Who were you with?

4. What was your reaction to the film?

5. Have you seen it since? What did you think of it that time?

Finally: Why do you think that was the film you remembered?

Notes: The list of films should include both classics and contemporary films, and be films that you are confident that members of your group will have seen, either in the cinema or on television (a look at the television schedules will provide the names of some that have recently been screened). Try to include films that you think may be of particular interest to group members; children's films are the most reliable, as they may have been seen either as a child or as an adult and parent. Allow for the fact that some group members may have seen their chosen film on video or television rather than in the cinema.

○ Children's books

Requirements: The names of a range of familiar children's stories on slips of paper, enough for each member of the group and the facilitators, and a couple extra to allow a choice. These should include some classics and some more recent titles, but they should be books that you are sure that members of your group will know. Suggested titles could include *Noddy, Little Women, Ballet Shoes, Charlie and the Chocolate Factory, Alice in Wonderland, Wind in the*

Willows, *Winnie the Pooh*, *Peter Pan* and the novels of Terry Pratchett and Roald Dahl.

Recommended warm-up: Describe your favourite children's book, and explain why that was your favourite story as a child.

Structure: Choose one of these titles.

1. When did you first hear this story? Where were you when you heard it?

2. Did anyone read it to you, or did you read it for yourself?

3. Were there any pictures in the book?

4. How did the story make you feel?

5. Have you come across this book since? What were the circumstances?

Finally: Why do you think that was the book that you chose to write about?

Notes: Be aware of cultural differences within the group, and acknowledge that European children's books may not be familiar to everyone in the group. This should be considered before the session, and the titles chosen according to the group membership. It would be possible to restrict the exercise to fairy tales, which will ensure more general recognition. (Alida Gersie and Nancy King's book *Storymaking in Therapy* is a useful resource for world fairy tales and should be investigated if you know that some group members have a different culture of children's stories.)

○ **Television/radio**

Requirements: None. Television and radio, as regular activities for most people, probably do not require prompts as some of these other exercises can; although the names of popular television programmes of the past and present on strips of paper, as in the 'Cinema' and 'Children's books' exercises, may be useful if the group or some group members are in need of a prop to encourage their writing. A list should include past programmes and some that are more recent, but they should be programmes that you are sure that members of your group will know and that take into account the age range of the members.

Recommended warm-up: What is your current favourite television or radio programme, and why?

Structure: Think of a television or radio programme that you enjoyed as a child or a teenager.

1. Name the programme, and describe what it was about.

2. Who was your favourite character or person in this programme?

3. What time of day was it on television or the radio? When did you watch it – when you came home from school, before or after supper? At weekends?

4. Where was the television or radio set? Describe the room in which you watched or listened to this programme.

5. Was there anyone around while you watched or listened to this programme, or did you watch/listen alone?

Finally: Is there a particular episode or occasion which stands out in your watching of this programme? Why do you think that this was the programme that you chose to write about?

Notes: Television viewing is a shared cultural knowledge, and this exercise is likely to produce shared nostalgia for favourite childhood programmes, which can be very productive in bonding group members together. Be aware of any member of the group who for reasons of age or cultural difference may not have shared the same programmes. It is important to include the option of radio, as some older group members may not have had access to television as children, and radio may have been more important to them. Include radio as a choice in the warm-up too; some people may choose not to have a television set.

○ **Fireplace**

Requirements: None.

Recommended warm-up: Describe a memory that you have of snow.

Structure: You are looking into a fire, and it is snowing outside the window. It may help to shut your eyes and imagine the fireplace.

1. Describe the fire. What do you see in the flames?

2. Describe the fireplace. Are there tiles? A grate? A mantelpiece?

3. Describe yourself sitting in front of the fire. What are you wearing? How old are you?

4. Look around you. Describe the room that you are sitting in.

5.   What is outside the window?

Finally: How does it feel to be sitting there?

Notes: This exercise may evoke childhood memories of being safe and secure and may produce negative associations; the possibility for both should be acknowledged. This is an exercise that works best in the winter, when it is cold and group members may be feeling particularly bleak. This exercise does assume that all the group members will have experienced snow, which may not be the case for those new to the country.

○ **Toys**

Requirements: None.

Recommended warm-up: Write down the name of a game you really dislike and explain why that is. Then, write down the name of a game that you really enjoy, and explain why.

Structure: Think of a toy that you spent a lot of time with as a child, and that was important to you – it could perhaps be a doll, a bear, a bicycle.

1.   Describe this toy and what it was that you particularly liked about it.

2.   Where did it come from? Did someone give it to you? If so, who?

3.   Did you share this toy with anyone? Did you play with it on your own, or with anyone else?

4.   When and how did it stop being important to you?

5.   What happened to it?

Finally: Why do you think that was the toy that you remembered?

Notes: This exercise is similar to the 'Games' exercise given earlier, but allows group members to describe a more private experience of playing. It is important to remember that not all group members will have had access to some of the toys that many children take for granted, or may have been unwillingly made to share a favourite toy.

○ **Pastimes**

Requirements: None.

Recommended warm-up: On a slip of paper, write down two unusual interests that you have now, or have had in the past. This warm-up can be extended into a game, in which the writers fold the slips up, and place them in the centre of the group. Each member then chooses a slip, and the group tries to identify which interests belong to which member.

Structure: Think of a pastime that was important to you as a teenager.

1.   How did you first become interested in this pastime?

2.   Describe what it involved, and how you spent your time.

3.   Did this pastime involve any specialist equipment, or magazines? If so, were you given them as presents, or did you have to buy things to support your interest?

4.   Did this pastime involve anyone else? Or did you pursue it on your own?

5.   What was your greatest achievement or most enjoyable moment in pursuing this pastime?

Finally: Looking back on it, why do you think that this was an activity you particularly enjoyed as a teenager?

Notes: This exercise can reveal unexpected aspects of group members. It is also a means of remembering forgotten skills and interests, and of focusing on an activity to which the writer was very committed and on a period of time at which they were capable of great conviction.

○ **Dens**

Requirements: None.

Recommended warm-up: What was your favourite place to go as a child?

Structure: Think of a space which was important to you as a child – somewhere where you spent a lot of time.

1.   Where was this place? Describe its location, and how you got to it.

2.   What was in this place? Were there special things that you kept there?

3.   Are there any special sounds or smells that you associate with this place?

4.   When did you tend to spend time there? Did you share it with anyone else, or was it a place that you went to by yourself?

5. Remember one particular time that you were in this place. What happened, and how did you feel?

Finally: What was it that was particularly special about this place?

Notes: Because this exercise focuses on private space and time in the past, it can promote painful and difficult memories, but it also works in the same way as the 'Safe place' exercise, in reminding people of a place that they remember as safe and secure.

○ **Pop stars**

N.B. This is an exercise which should be approached with caution. There can be cases in which a prominent musician who was once a teenage crush or who remains a fantasy figure in adulthood may have become the object of delusions. If you are aware of this in the case of any of the group members, it would be wise not to employ this exercise, and not to risk exacerbating the fantasy.

Requirements: None.

Recommended warm-up: What was the first record or tape that you bought for yourself, and why did you buy it?

Structure: Think of a musician or band whom you admired as a teenager.

1. Describe them. What did they look like, and what kind of music did they play?

2. What was your favourite song? Describe it, and explain why it was important to you.

3. Where did you listen to their music? Did you see them live, did you have their records or tapes? Did you listen to them alone or with friends?

4. How did you show that you admired them – did you have posters, or join a fan club, or dress like them?

5. What was it about this musician or group that appealed to you?

Finally: Have you listened to their music since? What do you think of it now? What became of the musician or band?

Notes: This exercise can generate a lively discussion about shared idols (and idols who are not shared!) and is a means of opening up an awareness of different fashions and tastes in music at different periods. This can develop into an appreciation of different tastes and a recognition of the different age and cultural allegiances within the group.

○ **First love**

Requirements: None.

Recommended warm-up: Identify three qualities that you look for in a person who may become important to you.

Structure: Remember your first love. This may be someone that you later did go on to know better, or may have been a crush on someone that you admired from afar. It might be someone famous whom you never actually met.

1. Who (or what) was the object of your first love? Briefly describe them and explain how it was that you knew them.

2. What was it that first struck you about them? Was it their appearance? Their clothes? Their personality?

3. Did you meet and get to know this person, or did you love them from a distance? Did you declare your feelings?

4. How did your feelings for this person become less intense? How did you move on from this first love?

5. What would you like to say to this person if you were to meet them now?

Finally: Is there anything that you would like to add about this person and your feelings for them?

Notes: This exercise may produce light-hearted reminiscence, or more painful memories. The option of writing about an adolescent crush allows the group members to choose to write about less intensely private experiences. It is important however to ensure that there is sufficient time at the end of the session to acknowledge any difficult feelings that might arise.

○ **First drink**

N.B. Some group members may have a very difficult relationship to alcohol, and you should be aware that this may be a very sensitive topic that may not be appropriate unless there is considerable trust within the group. Be aware too that there may be group members whose religion or cultural background does not permit them to drink – if this is the case, then this is not a suitable exercise for your group.

Requirements: None.

Recommended warm-up: What is your favourite drink, and why?

Structure: Think back to the first time that you drank too much alcohol; the first time that you can remember; or, if not the very first time, then think of a good story of an occasion involving alcohol.

1. What was the situation? Explain the occasion, and set the scene.

2. What was the drink? How did it taste?

3. How did it make you feel? How did you behave?

4. How did the event progress?

5. How did the event end? How did you get home?

Finally: Were there any consequences, or lessons to be learnt? How do you feel now looking back on the event?

Notes: Alcohol may well play a very important part in group members' lives, either by its absence or its presence. This exercise enables the group to look at early experiences of their relationship to alcohol and, in sharing what may be humorous stories, to examine their current relationship to it. This may provoke discussion about current attitudes towards drinking, and it is important to ensure that there is sufficient time to explore these with the group.

Painful feelings

The following exercises are designed to facilitate the exploration of negative memories and emotions, and provide a means of allowing these to be shared within the group. It is vitally important that the group should not be seen simply as a means of expressing positive feelings and memories, but as a forum in which it is possible to articulate difficult and painful emotions and thoughts. Although the previous set of exercises, 'Evoking the past', can bring up painful memories, the exercises in this section are specifically designed to focus on feelings of unhappiness, or on emotions that may be difficult to acknowledge. Again, these are exercises that should be employed at a stage in the group at which there is considerable mutual trust.

Asking members to write directly about painful memories and feelings is unlikely to produce anything other than very guarded and defended writing, but there are indirect ways of evoking such feelings and memories. There are generally shared experiences, such as the first day of school, which have provoked anxiety for most people and which can be beneficial for group members to recognise as commonly shared experiences. Some of these exercises allow for group members to write an imagined response to a person who may have hurt them in the past, and this is a particularly useful way of managing feelings of rejection.

Feelings that do not immediately appear as painful but which are familiar to everyone, such as boredom, can mask intense negative emotions and be a valuable means of exploring painful and unacceptable ideas. As in the 'Positive memories' section, there can be ambivalent responses to these exercises. It cannot be assumed that group members will choose to write about difficult feelings; they may prefer to write a positive account of the theme of the session.

◦ **First day at school**

Requirements: None.

Recommended warm-up: Write down three things that you enjoyed, and then three things that you hated about school.

Structure: Think back to your first day at school (either junior or senior school).

1. What were you wearing?

2. How did you get to school? Was anyone with you? Describe the journey.

3. Where were you taken when you first arrived at school? Describe the space.

4. Who are the people you remember most vividly?

5. What did you do at break time?

Finally: How did you feel at the end of the day?

Notes: This is a very good exercise for generating a feeling of community and of belonging within the group, as school is an experience that almost everyone has been through at some point in their lives. It is wise to ascertain that every group member has been through some kind of schooling before doing this exercise.

◦ **Hospital**

Requirements: None.

Recommended warm-up: What is your favourite medical series on television, and why?

Structure: Think of an occasion when you have been in hospital for a physical illness.

1. How did you get to hospital?

2. Describe your bed and the ward.

3. Who looked after you? Is there any doctor or nurse whom you remember particularly?

4. Who else was in the ward with you? Who did you talk to?

5. How did you spend your time?

Finally: How did it feel to be in hospital on that occasion?

Notes: This is an exercise to be handled with caution. Some of the group members may have had major operations themselves, or have had people close to them in hospital in a situation that will bring back extremely painful memories, and it is important to check whether this is the case. If this is not true of any member of your group, this is an exercise that could help group members to consider hospital as a place of healing, and to remember more positive aspects of a hospital's function.

○ **Boredom**

Requirements: None.

Recommended warm-up: Write down three things that you find really boring.

Structure: Think of a situation in which you have been really bored. This could be imaginary or real.

1. Where were you? What was the situation?

2. Describe the space that you were in.

3. Who was with you in this situation? Describe them.

4. What could you hear?

5. What were you doing? How else did you feel (apart from being bored)?

Finally: Was there anything you could have done to have made the situation less boring?

Notes: This is a session that is likely to produce a great deal of mutual recognition, and can produce some very funny writing. Nonetheless, it will become apparent from the writing that boredom can very often be used as a means to stifle anger. It is important to be aware of this, but whether or not facilitators should point this out will depend on the dynamic and stage of each group.

○ **Stranded on a train**

Requirements: None.

Recommended warm-up: Who is the celebrity you most dislike, and why?

Structure: You are stranded on a train with a person you dislike intensely (not known to the group). This can be someone famous, someone you know, or an imaginary figure.

1.   What is the situation – why are you stranded?

2.   How do you encounter this person? Describe them.

3.   How does conversation begin?

4.   How do you react to them?

5.   What happens next?

Finally: Is there anything that you'd like to say to this person while they are your captive audience?

Notes: This is playful and comic way of dealing with the expression of dislike for another person. The recommended warm-up will inject a note of humour into the session, as there are likely to be mutually detested personalities; another kind of warm-up could direct the session into a more explicit expression of dislike. It is important to direct the group away from writing about anyone who is known personally to the group, in order to avoid personal insult to any person who may be important to the group, or within the group itself. Some members of the group may find it difficult to express feelings of dislike directly, but in our experience, everyone has been able to think of somebody they disliked intensely. It is better to use the term 'dislike' rather than 'hate', as hatred can be a frightening concept.

○ **Teachers**

Requirements: None.

Recommended warm-up: Write down three things you enjoyed about school, and then three things that you disliked.

Structure: Think of a teacher that you remember well, either because you liked them particularly or disliked them very much.

1. Describe this teacher. What did they wear? How did they sound?

2. What subject did they teach, and what did it feel like to be in one of their lessons?

3. Describe something that this teacher said or did.

4. How did that make you feel?

5. Looking back, how do you feel about that teacher now? Is there anything that you would like to say to them?

Finally: Is there anything else that you would like to add about this teacher? Why do you think that they are the teacher that you remember?

Notes: This is an exercise that can produce both positive and negative memories of school life, but which can provoke feelings of resentment and bitterness. It is another exercise that generates a sense of mutual trust and recognition in the group, in that most people will have similar kinds of memories of school teaching.

○ **Friends and enemies**

Requirements: None.

Recommended warm-up: Write down three qualities that make someone a good friend, and three that would make someone a bad enemy.

Structure: Think of someone from your childhood who was a very good friend to you, or someone who was a very bad enemy.

1. Describe this person. What did they look like? What did they sound like?

2. How did it happen that they became your friend or your enemy?

3. How did they make you feel?

4. When was the last time that you saw this person?

5. What happened to this person? Or, if you don't know, what do you imagine became of them?

Finally: What would you like to say to this person now if you met them?

Notes: This can be a very good way of generating mutual support among the group members, in that everyone has a memory of a child who once made them miserable, or who was an important friend. It may be that not all group members will want to explore these feelings, and so it is important to allow for the memory of a positive childhood relationship.

○ **Irritation**

Requirements: None.

Recommended warm-up: Describe three things that you find extremely irritating.

Structure: Think of a recent incident (outside of the group) in which you found yourself very irritated.

1. Where were you? What was the situation?

2. Was there someone involved in this situation? Describe this person.

3. What were the circumstances that made you so irritated? Describe the build up to your irritation.

4. Did you express your irritation? If not, how did you feel?

5. How did the situation resolve itself?

Finally: How were you feeling before this situation, and how did you feel after it?

Notes: It may be difficult for group members to talk about being angry; they may find it easier to talk about feelings of irritation. This is another exercise that offers an oblique way into an expression of anger – the structure does allow for some reflection on the circumstances which provoke anger and for the writer's response to such situations, but the extent to which the group is prepared to discuss this will again depend on the dynamic and openness of the particular group.

○ **Threat**

N.B. This is another exercise that should be approached with caution. Please ensure that you have referred to the notes before embarking on it.

Requirements: None.

Recommended warm-up: Describe three things that frighten you, and explain why.

Structure: Think of a situation in which you have felt threatened.

1.   Where were you?

2.   What made you first aware of the threat?

3.   What happened?

4.   How did you react?

5.   How did the threat recede, and how did you cope afterwards?

Finally: How did you feel after the situation, and did you or anyone else make yourself feel better?

Notes: This is an exercise that should be handled with some care, as there may be members of the group who have experienced extremely violent behaviour or who have had violent hallucinations; it would be advisable to check records before embarking on this. That said, it can be beneficial, once a group feels safe with the facilitators and one another, to share their feelings of fear, to recognise these in each other, and also to acknowledge that are frightening situations which have been managed in the past. It would be a good idea to precede or to follow this exercise with the 'Safe Place' exercise in the 'Opening up' section in Chapter 2, in order to remind group members that they do have a sense of place in which they feel secure and unthreatened.

○ **First time**

Requirements: None.

Recommended warm-up: Write down three to five new skills that you have learnt. These could be anything from word processing to woodwork, cooking to Chinese.

Structure: Think of the first time that you did something on your own as an adult that you found difficult. This could be going to college, to work, to hospital – anything that later became a regular part of your life. Think back to your first day of doing it.

1.   Where did you go? How did you get there?

2.   Who did you meet first, and how did you introduce yourself?

3.   What were your first impressions of the place?

4.   What did you spend the day doing?

5.   How did you feel at the end of the day?

Finally: How did you experience things after this first day?

Notes: This is similar to the 'First day at school' exercise, and should therefore not be used in close proximity to that session, which will evoke similar feelings. It does, however, allow for a more adult experience of feelings of anxiety, and for a recognition that such anxiety at unfamiliarity is temporary and can be managed. The recommended warm-up here encourages a sense of confidence and a focus on the positive aspects of new experiences.

○ **Things I find difficult**

Requirements: None.

Recommended warm-up: Write down three things which you know you experience as being very difficult, and three things which you know you do well (you must have three of each).

Structure: Think of something that you find difficult and that you wish you could do better. This might be cooking, maths, singing, talking to new people – anything you cannot do well, but which some people can take for granted.

1. Describe this activity and how you go about it. How bad are you really?

2. What is it that makes you so bad at it?

3. Can you avoid doing this activity? If so, how? If not, how do you cope?

4. Can you disguise the fact that you are bad at it?

5. Are there any ways in which you could improve your ability, or steps you could take to make you less bad at it? Does it really matter that you can't do it well?

Finally: Why do you think you find this activity so difficult?

Notes: The warm-up should provide a mutual recognition that will make the main task of exploring group members' lack of competence in certain fields less threatening. Nonetheless, this is another exercise that requires a considerable amount of trust within the group, and the exercise should be introduced with an element of humour. It is important that facilitators are careful as to what they are prepared to admit!

CHAPTER 6

Empathy

The experience of mental distress can be exacerbated by feelings of social and personal isolation. The fact of being a member of a group and having to share personal memories and experiences in itself is challenging and potentially very beneficial, but those benefits can be extended by asking group members to consider other people and to write about relationships that are tangential or important in their lives.

These exercises are designed to develop empathy, and to facilitate an awareness of the experience, feelings and importance of other people (both imagined and real). This is an important aspect of creative writing, in that it demands an imaginative response beyond the immediately personal. The invention of a character is a means of perceiving from another point of view, and promotes an awareness of different lives and histories. These exercises are structured both to evoke a recognition of the influence of others, and to allow for an acknowledgement of different perspectives, which can enable very self-absorbed individuals to develop an awareness of their own impact upon other people. This kind of writing also encourages group members who may feel or who have felt very isolated to recognise that they do have a range of different kinds of relationships, and that there are important people in their lives.

○ **Shopping**

Requirements: None.

Recommended warm-up: What is your favourite shop, and why?

Structure: Think of a shop that you visit regularly. It can be a department store, or a local shop.

1. What is the shop's name, and what sort of shop is it?

2. What do you buy there, and when do you usually go there?

3. Describe a shopkeeper or sales assistant whom you see there. What do they look like, and what kind of person are they?

4. Describe that person's day in the shop, from their point of view.

5. Include your own visit to the shop, from the shopkeeper's point of view. What impression do they have of you?

Finally: Is there anything that this person would like to add about the shop and their experience of it?

Notes: This exercise is a good means of introducing the theme of relationships, in that it asks the group to consider a relatively unimportant relationship. The same principle could be extended and used in a range of different scenarios which involve everyday activities in public spaces (public transport, restaurants and libraries would be other examples). This exercise is similar to the 'Other people' exercise below, but allows group members to imagine another person's reaction to them, without it being somebody important to them.

○ **Jewellery**

Requirements: An exotic piece of jewellery that is not identifiable as belonging to the facilitators or to anyone known to the group.

Recommended warm-up: What is your favourite item of jewellery, or precious object, and why is it important to you?

Structure: Consider this item of jewellery.

1. Describe the piece of jewellery.

2. How was it made, and by whom?

3. Who does it belong to? Describe its owner.

4. How did they come to have it? Were they given it?

5. What does it mean to them?

Finally: Is there anything else that you would like to add about the piece of jewellery or its owner?

Notes: This exercise can employ any kind of exotic object, not necessarily jewellery. It is important to indicate that this object or piece of jewellery does not belong to anyone known to the group, in order to encourage an imaginative response. This is another exercise that prompts the creation of an invented character, and is a good way in which to introduce work that focuses on other people.

○ **Other people**

Requirements: None.

Recommended warm-up: Describe briefly someone (not known to the group) whom you see every day.

Structure: Think of a person whom you see every day, but who isn't known to anyone else here.

1. Describe this person briefly.

2. Write about the beginning of a day in the life of that person, in their words.

3. Introduce yourself into their day, still in their words.

4. How does their day end?

5. How do they think about you?

Finally: Is there anything about this person that you feel you have not yet said?

Notes: This is another exercise that should be deferred until a point at which the group is comfortable with one another, as it is quite demanding to ask people to think about others' perceptions of them.

○ **Flowers**

Requirements: A vase of flowers of any kind, but not one that will be familiar to the group.

Recommended warm-up: Describe an occasion on which you have had a bunch of flowers.

Structure: Imagine that these flowers are for you to give to the person of your choice.

1. Who is that person, and why do they deserve flowers?

2. What are the circumstances in which you would give them the flowers?

3. Is there anything that you would like to say to them when you give them the flowers?

4. How would they react?

5.   Why is that the person that you would choose to present with flowers?

Finally: Is there anything that you would like to add about this person?

Notes: This is an indirect way of asking the group to write about people who are important (or whom they would like to be important) in their lives, and therefore should be handled with some care. Time should be allowed at the end of the session for a discussion of feelings that may emerge.

○ **Admiration**

Requirements: None.

Recommended warm-up: Write down three qualities that you admire in yourself. Then write down three qualities that you dislike about yourself. You must have three of each.

Structure: Think of a person whom you admire. They can be someone you know, or a celebrity from the present or the past, or someone imaginary.

1.   Describe this person's appearance (if they are imaginary, make it up).

2.   Describe their character.

3.   Describe what is it about them that you admire.

4.   What qualities do they have that you would like to possess?

5.   Does this person have any dislikeable characteristics?

Finally: Is there anything that you would like to add about this person? Why are they the person you particularly admire?

Notes: Again, this is a means of asking group members to write about someone important to them, but it extends into a consideration of the qualities that are to be admired in other people. Asking the group to consider characteristics that may be less admirable also offers a way of avoiding an idealisation of another person, and of recognising that they may not be so very different from ourselves. The discussion could pick up on some of the qualities that were mentioned in the warm-up exercise. If the recommended warm-up could be too confrontational for your group, it can be adapted to refer to other people rather than the group members themselves.

○ **A first meeting**

Requirements: None.

Recommended warm-up: What would you do if you were making an arrangement for an evening with a good friend?

Structure: You meet someone for the first time at a party or public event – this person can be male or female, and can be a real or an imagined person.

1. Describe the event.

2. How does this person appear? Describe them.

3. How do you start to talk to them?

4. How do you lead the conversation to find out more about them?

5. What was it about this person that made you want to talk to them in the first place?

Finally: How do you make contact with this person again?

Notes: This may be a difficult exercise for those in the group who perceive themselves to be particularly shy, but the warm-up has already introduced the idea of friendship and provides a way into thinking about the need to initiate and to sustain friendships.

○ **Presents**

Requirements: None.

Recommended warm-up: Describe the present you would most like to be given. Money is no object, but it must be something that can be wrapped up.

Structure: Think of someone to whom you would like to give a special present.

1. What would you choose for them (again, money is no object, but it must be something that can be wrapped)? Why would it be appropriate to them?

2. Where would you go to buy it, and how would you choose it?

3. How would you wrap it up? Describe the paper and ribbon.

4. What card would you choose? What would you write on it?

5. What would the ideal circumstances be to give this present to this person?

Finally: What would their reaction be?

Notes: This exercise is clearly appropriate to Christmas, but could also be used to mark a birthday in the group or other festivals in which present giving is an important ritual. This is a useful way of deflecting past disappointments about special occasions, in that it focuses attention on to the pleasure of giving.

○ **Dinner party**

Requirements: None.

Recommended warm-up: Describe the best dinner you have ever had.

Structure: You have invited someone you like very much to dinner. Money for food and drink is unlimited, but you have to prepare it yourself.

1. What will you cook, and how will you prepare the dinner?

2. How will you arrange the table?

3. What drinks will you offer?

4. How will you arrange the room and the lighting?

5. How will you welcome this person into your house?

Finally: Is there anything else that you would like to provide for dinner or the setting?

Notes: Like the 'Presents' and 'Flowers' exercises above, this exercise deflects attention away from the writer on to the pleasure of preparing something nice for other people. The extent to which the group wants to explore the significance of the guest is up to the group, but it can be introduced by asking in the final section who this person is, and why the writer has gone to so much trouble for them.

○ **Problem page**

Requirements: Problem letters from magazine and newspaper problem pages, enough for each member of the group and the facilitators, and a couple extra to allow a choice. Be aware of the age and gender balance of the group, and choose the magazines and letters with that in mind.

Recommended warm-up: Think of a problem that you have recently experienced. Briefly describe what happened, and how you reacted.

Structure: Choose one of these problems, and think about your response to it.

1. What is your initial reaction to this problem?

2. Where do you think that the problem lies?

3. What resources does the writer have to deal with the problem – what help might be available to them?

4. What would you advise the writer to do?

5. Write a short response to the writer.

Finally: Is there anything else you think that the writer should do, that you were not able to include in your short reply?

Notes: This exercise can produce playful responses, but it also represents an important development from previous exercises in this section, in that it asks the group to engage with the problems of people unknown to them. It is advisable to check the problems against your own knowledge of the group members in order to avoid any that are too close to home and which group members may not be prepared to share with the group. This exercise can be empowering in asking the group to think about resources that might help, and the suggestions that emerge may well apply to problems that exist within the group. Ensure that there is enough time for a discussion in which these resources can be considered as options.

○ **Someone else's eyes**

Requirements: None.

Recommended warm-up: Think of someone that you have a good relationship with (who is not known to anyone else here). Describe what you like about them, and also any faults that they have.

Structure: Imagine yourself in that person's position.

1. Describe yourself through their eyes.

2. What characteristics do they value about you?

3. Is there anything that they find difficult about you?

4. How do you feel about the way in which they see you?

5. How would you like them to see you?

Finally: Are there any changes that you'd like to make in your relationship?

Notes: This is a demanding exercise – it can be threatening to be asked to think of yourself as others see you, although this idea has already been introduced in the 'Other people' and 'Shopping' exercises. It is important to include faults in the warm-up, so that the group members are reminded that those people who are friends or admired can also be imperfect. Ensure that you have some time left for discussion of the issues that arise for the group members before they leave the group, and to focus this on shared rather than individual concerns. It is also important that the subject of the exercise should not be known to the group, otherwise conflicts of loyalty and potential rivalries may arise among group members.

○ **Important people**

Recommended warm-up: Write down the name of a person who has been important in your life (anyone who is not known to the rest of the group). Describe them, and briefly explain why they have been important to you.

Structure: Think about this person, and think of writing a letter to them.

1. How do you begin your letter?

2. Now tell them why they are so important to you.

3. Explain to them the qualities that you like and value in them.

4. Thank them.

5. Now end your letter.

Finally: Is there anything else that you would like to say to this person?

Notes: Like the 'Presents', 'Flowers' and 'Dinner party' exercises above, this is a means of enabling group members to express their warm feelings for another person, and is a safe rehearsal for expressing them. It is important to specify that the person should not be known to anyone else in the group, as relationships between group members and hospital or institutional workers may be difficult and can be potentially rivalrous.

CHAPTER 7

Changes and Endings

Every group will go through cycles of beginnings and endings in which members and facilitators join or leave the group. There may be cases of serious illness or even death within the group, which should be acknowledged as important to the life of the group and its evolution, and marked in some way. The loss of a familiar person from the regularity of group meetings (for whatever reason) may bring up memories of other painful goodbyes, and the departure of a facilitator who has been a central figure in the group can be particularly difficult, although it may not be directly acknowledged as such by members of the group.

These exercises are designed for particular points of change, and should be referred to whenever there are significant changes or events in the structure of the group or in the lives of its members.

○ **I have been**

Requirements: None.

Recommended warm-up: Write down one job that you have enjoyed, and one job that you have very much disliked.

Structure: Write down all the different kinds of work that you have ever done in your life (including temporary or casual jobs).

1. What skills were involved in these jobs?

2. What were you good at?

3. What did you find very difficult?

4. Which of these jobs did you dislike most, and why?

5. Which did you enjoy most, and why?

Finally: How would you describe your working life now?

Notes: Although this is an exercise about introducing members to one another, and is a good way of marking the beginnings of a group, it should not be used in the very first weeks of a group. Group members may prefer to volunteer this kind of information once they are at a point of feeling comfortable with the group, rather than at the point of first meeting. The exercise allows group members to get in touch with their experiences and skills from the past, and is a very good way of learning more about the histories of members of the group. The group can often surprise themselves and each other with the extent and range of their experience, and allow themselves to feel some pride in their achievements. It is important to remember that not all group members will have had the experience of paid work, and to phrase the exercise in such a way that other forms of labour are validated.

○ Seasons

Requirements: None. This exercise can, however, be adapted with the use of postcards as prompts, if that is more appropriate to your group, in which case, a set of postcards (with a range of scenes, including views of the countryside and city scapes) could be provided, one for each member of the group and the facilitators, and a couple extra to allow a choice.

Recommended warm-up: Briefly describe the view that you see every day from your bedroom window.

Structure: Think of a view that you are very familiar with, and have known for some time. It may be the view from a window (you could use the view that you have written about in the warm-up exercise), a street scene, or a view from a park or a walk that you take often.

1. Describe this view as it looks at the moment.

2. Now describe how it looks in the height of summer.

3. How does it change in the depths of winter?

4. What are the distinctive features of this view as the seasons change?

5. What are the sounds that you associate with the view in each season?

Finally: What is it in this view that remains the same, whatever the season?

Notes: This exercise encourages the group to recognise change as natural and cyclical, and to acknowledge that there are elements which remain the same in any cycle of change. The wording of the stages should be adapted to the time of year in which you present the exercise.

○ **Twenty years on**

Requirements: None.

Recommended warm-up: Think back to ten years ago, to the year 19XX (fill in as appropriate). Write down some of the things that you remember as important to you in that year.

Structure: Imagine that you have entered a time warp, and find yourself 20 years ahead, in the year 20XX. A lot has changed in those 20 years.

1. Where and how do you live?

2. Describe the environment around you, and the ways in which the place you live has changed.

3. What kind of transport is available to you?

4. Are there any new technologies or inventions that have become part of your life?

5. How do you spend your time? What kind of work do you do?

Finally: What are your hopes and plans for the future?

Notes: This is a playful means of introducing the idea of the future and changes in the future, which can be very threatening. It allows group members to explore their hopes and ambitions, but it also allows an element of futuristic fantasy, which makes this less directly personal.

○ **Goodbyes**

Requirements: None.

Recommended warm-up: Write down three positive things about change and then three negative things (you must have three of each).

Structure: Think of a goodbye that you have had to say to an adult friend.

1. Who was this person? Why were they important to you?

2. What were the circumstances in which you had to say goodbye?

3. Where and how did you say goodbye to each other?

4. Have you kept in touch with this person?

5. What are your feelings about having to say goodbye from your perspective now?

Finally: Is there anything else that you would like to say about this person?

Notes: This may evoke a very painful memory for some members, and should only be used at a stage at which the group members have developed a real trust with one other and with the facilitators. It is appropriate to use when a long-standing member is leaving the group, but it is even more important if a facilitator is leaving; it allows the group to mark the occasion, and to recognise that there have been other significant farewells in their lives that they have been able to manage. Insisting that the warm-up should contain three good and three bad things about change allows the group to recognise that there are aspects of change that can be very positive, and this can be pointed out before the longer task begins.

CHAPTER 8

Imagined Worlds

These exercises are designed to encourage imaginative exploration, and ask group members to apply their creativity to the task in hand. This emphasis on the imaginative allows the group to acknowledge the importance and extent of their own creativity, and can help to enable group members to apply this to the events of their own lives. These exercises are useful to intersperse with the other groups of exercises, and can be used to break up an emphasis on painful or difficult feelings. They are also a means of introducing imaginative writing, and can serve to introduce the exercises in Chapter 11, 'Exploring literary form'; much of the work here could provide a jumping off point for more extended pieces of writing.

In asking the group to exercise their imaginations, these exercises invite them to explore aspects of themselves and their environment through a displacement onto a fantasy world. They are appropriate at a stage in the group at which members have developed some confidence in writing and a trust in the group. Although ostensibly about imaginary situations and responses, the responses the writers give can often be very revealing about their perception of their actual environment and their place in it. Be aware that for some group members an exploration of their imagination may feel overwhelming. These exercises should be used with care, and with a sensitivity to the individuals within the group. It is very important that these sessions include sufficient space for discussion at the end of writing, in order for the group to reorientate themselves in the present moment and context.

○ Room

Requirements: None.

Recommended warm-up: What is your favourite room? It can belong to you, or be another room that you know. Describe it briefly and explain why it is the one that you chose to write about.

Structure: Imagine a white space, with one door.

1. Describe the dimensions and the shape of this space. You can change the colour if you wish.

2. Add a window or windows. Is there anything hanging from the windows – curtains, or blinds?

3. Add furniture and features to the space – a fireplace, more doors, lighting?

4. Add decorations, pictures, mirrors, or anything else that you would like to be in your room.

5. How does it feel to be in this room?

Finally: Look around the room one more time. Is there anything else that you would like to add to your room?

Notes: This is a good exercise with which to introduce imaginative work into the group, as it is within the bounds of possibility, and is also a pleasurable fantasy. The way in which people choose to furnish their ideal space, with no limits, can also be remarkably revealing. It can be pointed out that this has produced an imagined setting which could be used as the beginning of a longer piece of writing.

○ **Island**

Requirements: None.

Recommended warm-up: Recall a view that really made an impression on you. Describe it, and how you came to be there.

Structure: You have come upon an uninhabited desert island.

1. Describe your island, the terrain and the surrounding landscape.

2. What do you do on your arrival?

3. Does your island have any particular features? Waterfalls? Rivers? Mountains?

4. Are there any animals there? Any particular birds?

5. Are there any communication links with the mainland? Do you have any visitors, or are you alone?

Finally: How does it feel to be on your island? Is there anything else that you would like to add about your island and the experience of being there?

Notes: This is a familiar fantasy from the radio programme *Desert Island Discs*, but is nonetheless revealing. The exercise could be expanded by adding the question 'do you make attempts to leave, or would you be happy to stay there?'

○ **Park**

Requirements: None.

Recommended warm-up: What is your favourite park, and why?

Structure: You have been invited to design a park, and are now sitting in the middle of your completed park on a bright spring day.

1. Describe where you are sitting.

2. Go for a walk. What can you see around you?

3. Describe the flowers and trees that you have chosen to plant. What colours and scents are there in your park? (Remember, this is your park, and it can be any colour you choose.)

4. Are there any special features that you have built into your park? Are there playgrounds? Fountains? A restaurant?

5. What are the rules for being in this park? Is there anything that people are forbidden to do, or anyone or anything that is forbidden to be there?

Finally: Describe the boundaries that mark out your park. What lies outside them?

Notes: This is an extension of the 'Garden' exercise in Chapter 9, but it refers to a public rather than a private space, and so the boundaries and regulations that writers impose upon their imagined space can be particularly revealing.

○ **Time machine**

Requirements: None.

Recommended warm-up: Which historical period would you most like to have lived in, and why?

Structure: You have access to a time machine that will transport you to whichever century you choose – in the past or in the future.

1. Where do you arrive?

2. The machine has provided you with appropriate dress. What are you wearing?

3. Who would you choose to meet? And how would you go about finding them?

4. What strikes you most about the period?

5. Is there anything that you would change?

Finally: Will you choose to stay, or will you return to the twentieth century?

Notes: This is another familiar fantasy from H.G. Wells' novel *The Time Machine*, and from numerous science fiction films and television narratives. It is, however, a useful way of introducing a historical perspective into the group, and of asking them to reflect on the advantages and disadvantages of their contemporary life.

○ **Making history**

Requirements: None.

Recommended warm-up: What is your favourite period in history, and why?

Structure: You have the power to turn back the clock and to change the course of history. You have arrived at a time and place outside your lifetime – think of what you would like to change.

1. What is the year? Where are you?

2. What is happening at this time?

3. How are you involved? What is your role in these events?

4. At what point do you use your power to change events? How does your power effect this change?

5. What are the consequences of your presence at that historical moment?

Finally: How will the history books write about these events now that you have changed them?

Notes: Like the 'Time machine' exercise above, this involves a historical dimension and is important in expanding the group's reference points beyond the here and now.

◦ **Theatre**

Requirements: None.

Recommended warm-up: Describe an occasion when you went to the theatre or to a live performance. What did you see and how did it make an impression on you?

Structure: Imagine yourself in a theatre – either real or imaginary. It can be any kind of theatre that you would like it to be.

1.   Describe this theatre space from the auditorium. Is there a curtain? What kind of seating is there? What sort of stage?

2.   Move on to the stage. What kind of scenery or set design is there? What is the lighting like?

3.   Introduce a character on to the set.

4.   Introduce another character.

5.   What is the first line? What happens next?

Finally: How would you develop your play? Give it a title.

Notes: This is another means of introducing the concepts of character, setting and narrative into the group, and of beginning to work with dramatic text. Be aware that going to the theatre may not be a familiar experience for every member of the group.

◦ **Famous people**

N.B. Please ensure that you have read the notes before using this exercise; it is not appropriate for any group members who may have delusional tendencies.

Requirements: None.

Recommended warm-up: List three to five famous people whom you like very much. They can be actors, musicians, politicians, writers, television personalities or sports people, but they should be alive. Explain briefly what you like about them.

Structure: Think of a famous person whom you would like to meet. They may be somebody from the list you have already made.

1.   Where would you choose to meet this person? You have unlimited funds to meet at the place of your choice. Describe the environment in some detail, even if you have never been there.

2. How do you present yourself? What do you wear and how do you feel?

3. How does the meeting progress? Include some of your conversation, and describe how you get on.

4. You discover something unexpected about this person. What is it?

5. How does the meeting come to an end?

Finally: How do you feel about this famous person now that you have met them?

Notes: This exercise has produced some entertaining results in our groups, and can be employed if the tone of the group needs some levity. If the group is at the point where its members are familiar with one another, the warm-up lists can be used in a game in which a facilitator reads out the separate lists and group members guess who wrote each list. As with the 'Pop stars' exercise in Chapter 5, it is important to remember that there may be cases in which a famous figure may be the object of a delusional fantasy.

○ **Paradise**

Requirements: None.

Recommended warm-up: Describe your favourite place in the world.

Structure: You have a magic carpet that rises into the air and transports you to your own paradise.

1. Describe the journey

2. Describe your arrival. What does your paradise look like?

3. Describe a period of time – an hour, or a day. What do you do in that time?

4. Does anything happen? Do you meet anyone?

5. You cannot stay. Describe returning to the carpet and your feelings on the journey home.

Finally: Will you return to this paradise and, if so, how will you ensure that you can get there again?

Notes: This is similar to the 'Island' exercise, although it is more fantastical and requires a return to everyday life. In discussion, the points of contact between the imagined paradise and the favourite place of the warm-up exercise could be brought out.

○ **Utopia**

Requirements: None.

Recommended warm-up: Where is the place that you would most like to be now?

Structure: You have been whisked to a planet which is inhabited, and have been given the task of designing a new society.

1.   Describe the landscape (you have the technology to make it anything you like).

2.   Who will inhabit this planet? What people would you like to live there, and who would you keep out?

3.   What are the rules for living on this planet? What would you have to do to be thrown off it?

4.   What kinds of work would people do? And what would you do?

5.   What kinds of leisure time and facilities would you plan for your planet's population?

Finally: What are the values that people live by on this planet?

Notes: This is a more extreme version of the 'Island' and 'Park' exercises. It asks people to design an ideal space, but allows group members to dream, articulating their own version of a utopia, and to consider social and political structures.

○ **Inventions**

Requirements: None.

Recommended warm-up: What do you think is the most important new technology to have arrived over the past ten years, and why has it been important to you?

Structure: You are in a position to develop an invention of your own.

1.   What would you like your invention to be able to do?

2.   Describe what it would look like.

3.   How would it work?

4. Now you can put your invention to work. Set the scene for its test
    run.

5. What happens? How do people react to your invention?

Finally: What are the consequences of your invention, once it has become
affordable and part of people's lives?

Notes: This is an exercise that also involves empathy, in that it asks the group to
consider the impact of their fantasy on other people, and to imagine something that
will be of social benefit.

CHAPTER 9

Opening Up

These are exercises which can be employed once the group members are familiar with one another and have built up a sense of mutual trust and confidence. These are more self-revealing than the other exercises, and are therefore inappropriate to the early stages of a group. It can be very tempting to interpret what group members have written, but it should be remembered that this may inhibit future writing, and may not be welcomed. The extent to which interpretations can be made should be guided by the group's own response (members may well choose to interpret their own as well as other people's work), and by the custom and practice of the group.

The last three exercises in this section encourage group members to reflect on their achievements and strengths. For those who have been in state of negativity about themselves, these can be among the most difficult and demanding writing exercises, and group members may be resistant to writing well of themselves. A good way of introducing these exercises is to use a warm-up in which the group are asked to list an equal number of positive and negative qualities about themselves, and to insist that there has to be an equal number of each. These exercises do serve to reinforce positive feelings, and to bring up previously unacknowledged attributes in the writer. They can also stimulate forgotten memories of past achievements, and allow for these to be publicly acknowledged.

It is important to be careful not to elicit more from group members than they are prepared to volunteer, and it is important to acknowledge and to support those group members who may be unwilling to articulate or to share their experiences. In such a situation (which has been rare in our experience) it can be suggested that such a member may like to stay and listen to other people's work, or to write without reading out what they have written.

○ **Typical day**

Requirements: None.

Recommended warm-up: Write about three things that you enjoy doing on a regular basis.

Structure: Think of a typical day in your life.

1. Where is it that you wake up? How do you get up?

2. What are your thoughts about the day ahead?

3. What activities do you do during the day?

4. Who do you meet in a typical day?

5. How do you spend the evening?

Finally: What are your last thoughts at the end of the day? For example, do you feel pleased, disappointed, tired?

Notes: This is a good exercise with which to introduce more open sessions, and grounds the group in a sense of the routines of each other's lives. It can be difficult for some group members who have a very low opinion of themselves and of their lives to have to confront what they may well see as a poverty of experience, and so this exercise should be delayed until a point in the group at which every member has a certain amount of confidence in revealing themselves through their writing. Nonetheless, the sharing of experiences is a means of promoting mutual support among group members.

○ **Haunts**

Requirements: None.

Recommended warm-up: Write down three things that you like about the area in which you live, and three things that you dislike (you must have three of each).

Structure: Think of your favourite place in the local area. It may be a street, park, pub, restaurant or cinema, but it should be somewhere that you go to regularly.

1. Where is this place? Describe what it is like.

2. When do you usually go there, and how often?

3. Do you go to this place alone, or with someone else? Are there any people that you meet there?

4. Describe the last time that you were there, or any particular occasion that stands out.

5. How does it feel to be in this place?

Finally: Why is this a place that you go to regularly?

Notes: This is another exercise that introduce the group to each other's regular routines but is relatively unthreatening, as it focuses on a public space. If for any reason a group member finds it difficult to write about somewhere they frequent outside their home, it can be adapted to include a space that they use at home.

○ **Room**

Requirements: None.

Recommended warm-up: What is your favourite object that you own? Why is it important to you, and why do you like it so much?

Structure: Imagine that you are taking a walk in your own room. No one is there but you.

1. Describe what the room looks and feels like.

2. What furniture is there?

3. What objects or pictures do you notice?

4. What is in this room that is particularly special to you? Or what do you least like about it?

5. What do you think this room says about you and the kind of person that you are?

Finally: How far, and in what ways, does this room represent you and your life?

Notes: This is another exercise that works to introduce the group to one another's everyday experience, but it moves into a description of a more personal space. It also allows the group members to describe objects that are important to them, and which may well have associated memories. It is important to recognise that some group members may only have had the experience of institutional rooms, and to devise means of drawing out the ways in which they have personalised these spaces. For this reason, you should also include the option of disliking aspects of the room, and acknowledge that group members may have very ambivalent feelings about the spaces that they live in.

○ **House**

Requirements: None.

Recommended warm-up: Think of a house that has been important to you in the past (it need not be your own house). Describe it briefly, and explain why it has been important to you.

Structure: Imagine a house – not a real house, but one that is your own invention. You have unlimited funds for building and decoration. Begin by writing: 'My house is…'

1. Describe the outside of your house. What kind of size and shape is it?

2. Enter your house. What is the hallway like, if it has one? Describe the light and the colour that you first encounter in the house.

3. Go into the main room. What kind of a room is it? What happens there? How is it decorated?

4. Find the bedroom, and explain how you get there. What kind of a room is it? How does it feel to be there?

5. Is there an attic or a basement in this house? What does it contain?

Finally: Describe what it feels like to be in your house.

Notes: This can be an unexpectedly revealing exercise in that it allows for the expression of a dream environment, and also because it enables a metaphorical unpacking of the basement or attic of the writer's mind.

○ **Garden**

Requirements: None.

Recommended warm-up: What is your favourite flower? What is special to you about it?

Structure: You are standing in front of a high wall with a door.

1. Describe the wall and the door.

2. You open the door on to a wide garden. What do you see in front of you?

3. Describe how the garden is planted. What are the dominant colours and shapes, and what kinds of flowers are there?

4. Are there any special features in your garden? Water? Trees? Statues?

5. How does it feel to be in this garden?

Finally: Take one final look around the garden. Is there anything else important that you would like to include?

Notes: It may be the case that some group members will have bizarre imaginings, and this is an exercise which can focus these into a more formal structure. While gardens will have positive associations for most people, it is important to recognise that some may choose to write about threatening and dangerous environments.

○ **Rose bush**

Requirements: None.

Recommended warm-up: What summer flower is most important to you, and why?

Structure: Think of yourself as a rose bush.

1. Where are you planted? By yourself, or are there other plants and trees around you?

2. Do you have leaves or thorns?

3. Describe your flower. What colour is it? Are there lots of petals, is it a bud, or is it an overblown rose?

4. What can you see from where you are?

5. Are you well looked after? Or are you a wild rose?

Finally: Is there anything else that you would like to add about your situation and environment?

Notes: This is a simplified version of an exercise that is sometimes used in Gestalt therapy. Although there can be an initial resistance to this leap of the imagination, the written results are very revealing about group members' sense of themselves and their place in the world.

○ **Building**

Requirements: None.

Recommended warm-up: What is your favourite public building, and why?

Structure: Imagine yourself as a building – any size or shape, but one that represents you.

1. What sort of building is it? Where is it situated?

2. What goes on in this building? Who or what is located in it?

3. What sort of character does this building have? Is it a pleasant and welcoming building, or is it elegant and stand-offish?

4. How does this building view the world?

5. Stand back and look at this building. How do you feel looking at it?

Finally: Is there anything that you would like to add about your building?

Notes: Again, this is an oblique way of inviting the group members to write about themselves and their self-perception.

○ **Moods**

Requirements: None.

Recommended warm-up: Write down six to ten words that come to mind and which describe the dominant moods and emotions in your life at the moment.

Structure: Think about the mood that dominates your life at this moment.

1. Describe this mood, and how it feels to experience it.

2. How does this mood affect the way in which you see the world around you?

3. Does it affect your relationships with other people? If so, how?

4. Does this mood dominate or take over from other feelings?

5. What, if anything, breaks this mood?

Finally: Are there any other feelings that are associated with this mood?

Notes: This is an exercise that requires considerable trust within the group; nonetheless, it can be beneficial for members to describe their dominant state of mind, and to have this publicly acknowledged. This is an exercise which could usefully be extended into a dramatic dialogue, based on fact or fiction, and so allow for further exploration of the emotions that have been articulated. If there is no time for this, it is important to allow time to discuss the feelings that have emerged in the course of writing before the session ends.

○ **Blind date**

Requirements: None.

Recommended warm-up: Describe an arrangement you would make for your ideal romantic evening out (money is no object).

Structure: Start by imagining an advertisement in a lonely hearts column.

1. Write a few words which describe the advertiser (who can be real or imaginary) for their advertisement.

2. Now describe their ideal partner (real or imaginary) in the same advertisement.

3. Now write a reply to the advertisement from that partner, in which they describe themselves and their interests.

4. Now describe the advertiser's response to that letter describing themselves and their interests.

5. What happens next? Do they meet? If so, what arrangement do they make?

Finally: How do you think this relationship might develop?

Notes: This exercise may be close to the bone for any member of the group who has placed such an advertisement, or who may have considered it. However, the option of a real or imagined advertiser allows group members the claim that this is an entirely fictional situation. It could also be stressed that it is perfectly possible to approach this exercise in a humorous way, which allows group members to distance themselves. For those in the group with partners, this may be particularly important.

○ **Station**

Requirements: The names of major railway stations clearly written on slips of paper, enough for each member of the group and the facilitators, and a couple extra to allow a choice. It is a good idea to have the option of some cities or towns that you know to have particular associations for group members – a home town for example – but also some relatively innocuous places associated with holidays, such as Brighton or Blackpool.

Recommended warm-up: What is your favourite railway station, and why?

Structure: Choose one of these stations – one that has particular associations for you.

1. You've arrived at this station. Describe what you see in front of you.

2. You walk from the station into town. What do you see on the way?

3. Where are you going? Why?

4. You arrive at your destination. Describe your arrival and the surroundings.

5. Does this place have any associations or memories for you?

Finally: How does it feel to be in this place again?

Notes: This exercise can produce both happy and unhappy memories and associations, and the choice of stations will have much to do with this.

○ Safe place

Requirements: None.

Recommended warm-up: Describe three things that make you feel safe and secure.

Structure: Think of a space in which you feel safe. It can be an imagined or a real place.

1. Describe this space.

2. Are you aware of any sounds?

3. What things do you have around you in this place?

4. Is it a private space, or do you share it with anything or anyone?

5. How do you feel being in this place – apart from safe?

Finally: What is it about this space that makes you feel so safe?

Notes: This would be a good exercise to undertake before the 'Threat' exercise in Chapter 5, as it allows the group to recognise that they do have spaces which they have created for themselves in which they can feel secure.

○ Myself

Requirements: None.

Recommended warm-up: Write down three things that you like about yourself and three things that you dislike (you must have three of each).

Structure: Think about the characteristics in yourself that you have just listed.

1.   What impact do these qualities have on your life?

2.   What do other people like about you?

3.   What qualities in you would you like to keep?

4.   What things about you would other people like to see changed?

5.   What things would you like to change in yourself?

Finally: Is there anything else that you would like to add about your qualities?

Notes: This is an exercise designed to ask group members to consider their positive qualities, and to recognise the possibility of change. It is an exercise that many people will find threatening. It can be very difficult for those who are feeling negative about themselves to acknowledge any positive qualities publicly, and this exercise should not be attempted before there is a considerable measure of trust within the group. If you have a sense that there are members of your group who will resist writing about themselves, a supply of pictures or photographs of unknown people, so that the same exercise can be displaced on to an imaginary person, can be an option for both the main task and the warm-up exercise.

○ Achievement

Requirements: None.

Recommended warm-up: Briefly write about two or three things that you enjoy, and two or three things that you are good at. These may overlap.

Structure: Think of a recent achievement – something that you have accomplished and of which you are proud.

1.   What was this achievement, what was involved in it, and where and when did it happen?

2.   What preparation did you have to make beforehand?

3.   What was it that made you want to do this?

4.   Did you accomplish it alone, or were there other people involved?

5.   What was the biggest difficulty that you encountered, and how did you overcome it?

Finally: What can you learn about yourself through this achievement?

Notes: Again, because this exercise concentrates on positive aspects, it is something that many group members who are in a negative frame of mind may find difficult. It is important to stress that every group member will have achieved something, and to emphasise that each achievement stands on its own merits, no matter how small it may seem to the writer.

If there are problems in your group with long-term memory, it can be helpful to break this exercise down over two (or even more) sessions, and to invite contributions from the very recent past, and then from the more distant past, perhaps which involve more significant events. Inviting achievements from the previous two weeks helps as a prompt to the memory, and can also serve as an orientation towards longer-term projects, while asking for contributions from the past year (or longer), allows for the opportunity to discuss potentially more important life achievements.

○ **Strengths**

Requirements: None. For some groups, prompt cards may be helpful, which could list qualities that you have identified in members of the group. These might include courage, humour, intelligence, patience, kindness.

Recommended warm-up: Think of three qualities that you value in yourself or in other people, and briefly explain why you think that they are important.

Structure: Think of a situation when you had to make use of one of those qualities.

1. What was the situation, and where did it take place?

2. Describe the setting. Who was there and what was happening?

3. How were you involved and what did you do?

4. How did other people react to the situation?

5. How did you feel immediately afterwards?

Finally: Looking back on the situation, how do you feel now about what you did?

Notes: This exercise can stimulate memories of past achievements which have been left untold, and allows each member to recognise that they have important personal qualities and have made contributions which are to be valued. Be aware that there may be different definitions and emphases on particular qualities within the group, for example, looking after oneself might be construed as selfish by some group members, and for others could be seen as a positive strength. These are issues that can be explored in a discussion.

○ **Ideal me**

Requirements: None.

Recommended warm-up: Think of a historical figure whom you admire, and explain what it is that you find impressive about them.

Structure: You are in a position to lead your ideal life. This can be based in reality, or can be entirely fantasy; you can live anywhere and at any time that you choose. You may have won the lottery, found the job of your dreams, or live in another historical period.

1. Describe your ideal appearance. How do you look and how do you dress?

2. Where do you live? What is your house like?

3. How do you spend your time?

4. What are the things that you value the most in this ideal life?

5. What are your dreams and aspirations for the future?

Finally: How does it feel to live this ideal life?

Notes: While allowing the group to explore fantasy lives, this exercise also allows for some reflection on things that are to be valued in the group members' current lives.

CHAPTER 10

General Themes

These are useful exercises in that they can be slotted into any moment within the group's life and can also be used to mark particular seasonal or important social moments. They also employ a range of different writing styles; they incorporate both poetry and prose forms, and can therefore be used to vary the experience and to develop the writing skills of the group.

It is important to acknowledge that religious or other kinds of festival may not always be marked or celebrated in the same way by all group members, and to recognise and to allow for cultural, religious and ethnic difference. Some festivals, however, such as Christmas, are culturally unavoidable and may bring up feelings and memories that may be difficult to articulate in another context, but which may be of great importance to group members.

○ **Walk**

Requirements: None.

Recommended warm-up: What is your favourite place for a walk?

Structure: You are standing in the open air, in a place you have never been to before, with a path stretching out in front of you.

1. What can you see ahead of you?

2. Walk down the path a little. Does the landscape change?

3. You come to a hillside, and cannot see the other side. Describe the hill as you climb up it.

4. You reach the top of the hill. What can you see in front of you?

5. How do you feel being there?

Finally: How do you get down from the hilltop? Or do you choose to stay there?

Notes: This is an imaginative exercise that can be adapted for any time of the year. Including a reference in the introduction to the current weather, such as 'it is a bright cold day' or 'it is a very hot day', will give the exercise an immediacy.

○ **Summertime**

Requirements: None.

Recommended warm-up: Describe three things that you enjoy about very hot weather, and three things you dislike.

Structure: You are lying outside in the sun and it is very hot. Your eyes are shut.

1.   What can you feel physically?

2.   Open your eyes. What can you see above you?

3.   What sounds can you hear?

4.   What smells are you aware of?

5.   Are you alone, or are you aware of other people?

Finally: How does it feel to be lying in this place?

Notes: It is important not to assume that all group members will have had the experience of a beach holiday and for the facilitators to try to avoid writing about any enviably exotic or luxurious holiday they may have had; lying in the garden should be taken as an equally valid response to this exercise.

○ **Music**

Requirements: A tape recorder and a prepared tape with a selection of four or five brief extracts of different kinds of music. Your group and their age range will determine the kind of music that you choose, but the pieces should not be immediately identifiable, and should be very different from one another. They might include jazz, classical, brass bands, popular songs and at least one piece of abstract or atonal music.

Recommended warm-up: Think of a piece of music that is important to you, and explain what it means to you.

Structure: Listen to each of these pieces of music. Think about your responses to them.

1. Jot down a set of words that you associate with each piece of music.

2. Do you associate any particular colours with each piece?

3. What images does each piece evoke for you?

4. Do any of these pieces of music provoke any particular memories?

5. What feelings does any one of these pieces of music arouse in you?

Finally: Which piece of music do you find the most evocative, and why?

Notes: Music is a very powerful source for provoking memory and feelings, and this exercise could be extended by inviting group members to bring in music that has been important to them to share with the group and to use as the basis for a piece of writing. The lists of words could be structured into a poem.

○ **Scents**

Requirements: A selection of different oils, herbs, perfumes and other evocative smells. These could be in unmarked small bottles or put on to tissues.

Recommended warm-up: What is your favourite scent, and why?

Structure: Write down your responses to these scents.

1. Write down a set of words that you associate with each scent.

2. Do you associate each scent with any particular colours?

3. Do these scents evoke any images for you?

4. Do any of the scents bring back particular memories?

5. What feelings do you have in smelling any one of these scents?

Finally: Which scent do you find the most evocative, and why?

Notes: Smell is, like music, another powerful means of evoking memories. As for the music exercise, this exercise could be extended by inviting each group member to bring in a scent that has been important to them, and to use as the basis for a session.

◦ **Christmas**

Requirements: None.

Recommended warm-up: Write down three things that you enjoy about Christmas, and three things that you dislike (you must have three of each).

Structure: You are Father or Mother Christmas. You have magical powers, unlimited funds and the ability to travel anywhere at great speed. This year, instead of the traditional Father Christmas, you are the real one. You do not have to follow any set rules.

1. Where do you live and work? Briefly describe the room you work from.

2. You have a duty to deliver presents around the world once a year, but the choice of them is up to you. What do you have in your (bottomless) sack?

3. What is your choice of transport? (Remember you have magical powers.) How will you deliver the presents?

4. How do you decide who will get presents (and – if you like – who doesn't)?

5. How will you relax at the end of Christmas Eve?

Finally: Is there anything else that you feel it is important to do to mark Christmas?

Notes: This is a way of acknowledging Christmas, without emphasising the religious aspects of the festival. It is important to recognise that not all members of the group will celebrate Christmas, and to acknowledge that for some it may be a particularly difficult time, but the focus of this exercise deflects away from potential disappointments on to the pleasure of giving.

◦ **Fireworks**

Requirements: None.

Recommended warm-up: What is your favourite kind of firework and why?'

Structure: A firework manufacturer has asked you to develop a firework which expresses you and your personality.

1. Describe its packaging and shape.

2. What does your firework do? Is it a rocket? A wheel? Can it be held in the hand?

3. What colours does it have?

4. What sounds does it make?

5. Give it a name.

Finally: Are there any other features that you would like to add to your firework?

Notes: Although this exercise is clearly associated with Guy Fawkes night, it is important to remember that this is a particularly English and Protestant event, and that any Catholic member of the group might well not see it as an occasion for celebration. While acknowledging this, it can be presented as a festival which has largely been divested of its overt religious and political significance and which has become a public event for those living in England. It can be emphasised that fireworks are not only used on 5 November, but to mark all kinds of events.

○ **Bonfires**

Requirements: None.

Recommended warm-up: Describe an occasion you remember which had a bonfire at its centre.

Structure: Think of the bonfire.

1. Write a list of five colours you associate with a bonfire.

2. Write down five words that describe the smells of a bonfire.

3. Write down five words that describe the sounds that a bonfire makes.

4. Write down five objects that you would associate with an event that involved a bonfire.

5. Write down five tastes that you might encounter at a bonfire event.

Finally: Turn the words that you have listed into a structured piece of writing, which can be either prose or poetry.

Notes: As for the firework exercise above, this is clearly appropriate for the week of 5 November, but again, it should be stressed that the exercise is not restricted to those nights, but could be about any event involving a bonfire.

○ **Politics**

Requirements: None.

Recommended warm-up: Write down the word 'Politics'. Now write down ten words that you associate with the subject.

Structure: Think of a political event which stands out in your memory.

1. What is it, and when did it occur?

2. Describe what happened. What were the circumstances of this event, and who were the key players?

3. How did you hear about it, and where were you at the time?

4. How did you react? What were your feelings, and did you do anything?

5. How did the media react? What was the general public reaction? Was your reaction different?

Finally: What was it about this event that made an impact on you?

Notes: This is a useful exercise at times of elections, or when there are significant world events. It encourages an engagement and response to political structures and movements and to a world beyond the confines of the group. Be aware that this exercise may promote political differences within the group, and should therefore be used at a stage when the group members are familiar and comfortable with one another and in a position to tolerate political difference. It is not, however, advisable for facilitators to declare their own political allegiances too directly, or in their writing to choose an event that reveals too much about their own political convictions. This exercise could be extended by asking the group to write about the event they have described as if they were a journalist.

○ **Celebrations**

Requirements: None.

Recommended warm-up: List all the days of the year which have a special significance for you, such as anniversaries, birthdays and festivals. Which of these are personal to you, and which are celebrated by society as a whole?

Structure: Think of a special occasion which is important for you to celebrate. This may be a festival, anniversary, or your birthday.

1. What is the date, and what is it that is being celebrated on this day?

2. How do you celebrate this day? How is it typically celebrated? Do you do anything that is different?

3. Describe any important images or sounds that you associate with this day.

4. Do you eat any special food on this day? Are there smells and tastes that you particularly associate with this celebration?

5. Describe a particular occasion when you celebrated this event, and explain why that is the time that stands out for you.

Finally: Is there anything that you don't like or find difficult about this celebration?

Notes: This exercise can be used to mark events such as the birthday of a group member, or the anniversary of the group. It is important to include the final stage, and to acknowledge that days of celebration can be experienced as difficult or lonely, and can provoke feelings of loss and sadness.

CHAPTER II

Exploring Literary Form

These are more formal 'literary' exercises that borrow from established literary forms. They are not exercises to be used at the beginning of a group's formation, in that they can evoke associations of school English lessons and so be intimidating. But as a group develops confidence, these exercises are useful in allowing group members to experiment with writing and also to become accustomed to formal constraints on their work. Paradoxically, these imposed limits can help to facilitate creativity. It is nonetheless important to judge the group members' capabilities, and not to impose a structure too early in the group's development that some members may find over-demanding. It may be that group members get stuck with a particular line and are unable to continue. In this situation it is appropriate to suggest that they either write notes, incomplete sentences, or nonsense; asking them to continue writing within the structure (even if it is gibberish) means that they will get a sense of the form. Creative writing books written for students (some of which are listed in the 'Useful books' section in the appendices) will be full of ideas for forms that can be adapted for use with your group. Emphasise to the group that poetry does not have to rhyme; many of these exercises take the form of free verse.

A particularly good way of introducing the group to poetic form is to borrow an idea from an established poet and then to structure it into an exercise that follows the pattern of previous work and with which the group is familiar. It can be very productive, although not essential, to have copies of the work on which such an exercise is based, and to distribute them after the reading of the group's own work at the session. It is important not to reveal these before the group have written their own responses, as this might suggest that there is a 'correct' way of responding to the task, and may well inhibit a creative and imaginative response. Having another poet's work to look at in the group is nonetheless a very good means of encouraging the reading of other poets, and of demonstrating that the work done in the group has precedents. This kind of exercise also offers a means of introducing the group members to poems and to poets that they might not otherwise have considered reading.

○ **Taliesin**

(with thanks to Barry Palmer)

Requirements: None.

Recommended warm-up: Take yourself back to the past. Jot down a list of images of yourself as a child, a teenager, an adult – both good and bad – that occur to you. Include the things that you imagined yourself being, the things that you felt, and the things you thought you were. You can also use symbols and real things to evoke a sense of yourself.

Structure: Write the line: 'I have been' and add an image from your list. Go on to write eight or ten more lines, each of which begins 'I have been' and which adds another image from your list. The lines do not have to rhyme.

Finally: End the poem with a final line. If you do not have a line you particularly want to use, you can write the line: 'All these things I have been.'

Notes: Taliesin (the bard) was an early twentieth-century Welsh poet who developed this form of poem. This is an excellent means of introducing poetry to the group, in that the very simple form is undemanding, but still requires members to contribute personal images from their past (see Pennar 1988).

○ **Martian**

Requirements: A number of slips of paper with ordinary household objects clearly written on them, enough for each group member and the facilitators, and a couple extra to allow a choice. Suggestions might be a kettle, an iron, a television, a radio, a computer, a car. Copies of Craig Raine's poem 'A Martian Sends a Letter Home' (Raine 1979) are useful but not essential to have to hand.

Recommended warm-up: Choose one of these objects, and describe it as if you had never seen it before, to someone who does not know what it is.

Structure: You've just been teleported into this room from a spaceship. You have never seen people, or any of these things before. You must send back a log of your findings (as you have landed in an English-speaking country, your language will be English).

1. Write notes on the shapes and colours that you see. Make notes on the quality of light and the temperature.

2. Identify an object in the room, and explain its function.

3. Are there other objects that you think it is important to note?

4. What are the rules that it is important to understand in this world?

5. Describe your impressions of the human beings in the room and their behaviour.

Finally: Is there anything else that you think is important to tell your mother ship about this world that you have landed in?

Notes: This is an adaptation of Craig Raine's poem 'A Martian Sends a Postcard Home'. It is a good exercise for developing observation and, because it is a playful idea, is appropriate for early stages in the group. The exercise can be written up as a poem, but this is not necessary – it will stand up as an exercise in observation however it is written.

○ These I have loved

(with thanks to Barry Palmer)

Requirements: Copies of Rupert Brooke's poem, 'The Great Lover' (Rogers 1987) are useful to have to hand, but not necessary.

Recommended warm-up: Write a list of six of your favourite things in the world.

Structure: Begin by writing the line 'These I have loved...'

1. In a short line, describe one of your favourite things and what it looks like.

2. Add another line that describes your favourite sound.

3. Add another line that describes your favourite smell.

4. Add another line that describes your favourite taste.

5. Add another line that describes the sensation of touching something.

Finally: Finish by writing a last line. If nothing else comes to mind, you can use the line 'All these have I loved'.

Notes: This exercise is taken from a section of Brooke's poem 'The Great Lover', which might be appropriate to show to the group after their own writing. The above five lines are based on the senses, and with the opening and closing lines will make a concise poem. This exercise need not be as prescriptive as outlined above, and there is nothing to stop members adding as many lines as time and their invention will allow.

○ **Does she like…**

Requirements: Copies of Wendy Cope's poem 'Does She Like Word Games?' (Cope 1988) are useful but not essential.

Recommended warm-up: Six things you like (anything at all, from music to food) and six things you dislike.

Structure:

1. Write a line as follows, and fill in the blanks from your list (or, if you prefer, add new ideas): 'She (or he) likes… but she (or he) doesn't like…'

2. Write another line in the same way, using two different things from your list.

3. Now write two lines beginning: 'She (or he) likes…'

4. Now write two lines beginning: 'She (or he) doesn't like…'

5. Now write two lines beginning: 'Her (or his) favourite…'

Finally: Write two lines to finish the poem.

Notes: This is based on a poem by Wendy Cope. It is a playful way to introduce poetry, and is very close to the listing exercises that the group is familiar with from warm-up exercises. Having the poem to hand will demonstrate what can be done with very simple word games.

Further work with poetry

These are more demanding exercises, which should be introduced at a point in the group where members have some experience of writing, and some familiarity with the structure and constraints of poetic form. This does not mean that the group needs to be very advanced in their understanding of literary conventions – these are all exercises that are accessible to people who are relatively new to writing, but the requirement to frame pieces of language into a structure frame, or, in some cases, the strict nature of the form may prove initially intimidating to inexperienced members of the group.

○ Haiku

The haiku originated as a Japanese form in the seventeenth century, in which three short lines catch an image. It is a deceptively simple poetic form, but its brevity and strict regularity makes it an appropriate way of introducing poetry into the group. The form can be introduced as a development from the work of listing words that has often be used as a warm-up.

Requirements: Photocopied examples of the haiku form are useful, but not essential. For example:

Snow drifts though the sky

Greyish clouds open

Cat finds warm burrow

Recommended warm-up: Write down three things that are associated with the chosen theme of the haiku and of the session. This theme may be to do with the seasons or with an abstract concept, such as change, time, youth or age. The chosen theme may well have already informed the group's work in other exercises.

Structure: Technically, the structure of the haiku is three lines, in which the first has five syllables, the second, seven, and the last five. The haiku does not rhyme, and is usually about a theme such as time passing or the seasons. In English, it is not necessary to worry about the exact number of syllables, lines of similar lengths will do.

Introduce the rhythm of the haiku by reading an example to the group, emphasising the syllables. This may have to be repeated several times, until everyone in the group is confident with the formal structure of a haiku.

Introduce the chosen theme, and ask the group to write one line of five syllables, one of seven, and then another of five, while stressing that the exact number is not important.

Notes: The haiku is a very short form of poetry, but its difficulty should not be under-estimated; some group members may prove more adept at the form and the exercise may take some people longer than others. It may well be that the time will allow for two or more themes to be worked on, and that these should be offered to those who have completed a first haiku.

○ **The seven joys of autumn**

(with thanks to Barry Palmer)

Requirements: Copies of Ted Hughes' poem 'The Seven Sorrows of Autumn' (Hughes 1975) are useful but not essential.

Recommended warm-up: Write down a list of words (at least seven) of things that you enjoy about this time of the year. Include scents, colours, tastes and sensations.

Structure: Begin by writing 'The first joy of autumn is…'

1. Now, incorporating one of the things on your list, write a two line sentence describing that aspect of autumn.

2. Now write 'The second joy of autumn is…', and write another two lines using another word from your list.

3. 'The third joy of Autumn is…' – add another two lines.

4. 'The fourth joy of Autumn is…' – add another two lines.

5. The fifth joy of Autumn is…' – add another two lines.

6. The sixth joy of Autumn is…' – add another two lines.

7. The seventh joy of Autumn is…' – add another two lines.

Finally: Write a final line. If you are not inspired, then write 'These are the seven joys of autumn'.

Notes: This exercise is borrowed and adapted from Ted Hughes' poem 'The Seven Sorrows of Autumn'. It need not be limited to Hughes' autumn, but could be adapted to the seven joys of spring, summer or winter. It is also possible to write or to rewrite the same exercise as the seven sorrows, which is the actual title of Hughes' poem. Explain that Hughes' poem is written in free verse.

○ **Sonnet**

Requirements: Copies of a sonnet are useful to have to hand, but not essential. It is more important (although again, not essential, if the facilitator's verbal instructions are very clear) to have a sheet marked up with the rhyme scheme of the sonnet form, and with the 14 lines numbered, as follows:

1   a

2   b

3   a

4   b
5   c
6   d
7   c
8   d
9   e
10 f
11 e
12 f
13 g
14 g

These should be given out before the main exercise, and can be used to explain the structure.

Recommended warm-up: What is your favourite poem, and why?

Structure: The sonnet has a very strict format: it is 14 lines with a fixed rhyme pattern. It is based on a single theme which develops into a final rhyming couplet. Rather than introducing the rhyme pattern at the beginning, it is less intimidating to instruct in stages, and to indicate when to rhyme at the beginning of each line. If you do not have marked-up sheets, ask group members to write numbers from 1 to 14 down one side of their paper. Group members should be warned to consider that every word with which they finish a line has to find a rhyme.

1. Give the group a first line. One borrowed from a familiar poem works well, as long as it refers to a common experience. A line from Coleridge's 'Frost at Midnight' – 'How oft at school with most believing mind…'– (Gardner 1972) or from Shakespeare's Sonnet XV – 'When I consider every thing that grows…' – (Craig 1972) are both good starting lines; they are sufficiently general and refer to experiences which should be familiar to most people.

2. Now ask the group to write a line that follows on from this first line.

3. Write a line in which the last word rhymes with the last word of the first line.

4. Now write a line in which the last word rhymes with the last word of the second line.

5. Write a new line, continuing the theme and the sense of the poem.

6. Add another line.

7. Now write a line in which the last word rhymes with the last word of the fifth line.

8. Now write a line in which the last word rhymes with the last word of the sixth line.

9. Write a new line, continuing the theme and the sense of the poem.

10. Add another line.

11. Now write a line in which the last word rhymes with the last word of the ninth line.

12. Now write a line in which the last word rhymes with the last word of the tenth line.

13. This is the first line of the final couplet, in which you can introduce a new rhyme.

14. Write a final line that rhymes with the line above.

Notes: Although the sonnet is an apparently very difficult form, its strict regularity does mean that most group members can manage it, as long as the instructions are made very clear. It is therefore very important that facilitators have a clear grasp of the form before they begin the session. This is an exercise that can either be undertaken individually or collectively, in which case each member of the group begins a sonnet and then circulates the paper after each line. A collective sonnet is a good way of introducing the group to more demanding forms of poetry and may give the members the confidence to develop their own sonnet.

Guidelines for Adapting or Creating
Your Own Exercises

The success of these exercises will very much depend on your client group, and on your own experience and skills in judging the mood of the group. You may well find that your own group reaches a point at which issues not covered in this handbook need to be addressed. You may work through some of these exercises, get a sense of their structure, and then move on to invent your own, to suit the particular needs of your group. This collection can act as a reference point from which you can develop your own ideas, based on your knowledge of the individuals and processes within your own group.

It has been our experience that the most productive sessions of writing emerge out of highly structured exercises in which the group members are taken through a piece of writing step by step. These steps nudge the writer into the next stage of writing, and help to offset anxiety at the prospect of writing a long piece of prose. The stages can also facilitate a more thorough exploration of the theme of the session, and prompt material that might otherwise have been lost. A set of five stages will cover an hour's session, leaving time for the reading out of work. If you have a longer or shorter session, or if you have a small or very large group, exercises can be reduced to four stages, or expanded indefinitely.

There will inevitably be individuals within the group who feel restrained by this format, and there can be moments at which the entire group will resist the structure of the session. In these cases, it is possible to relax the framework, and to introduce free sessions of writing which are organised more loosely around a common theme. It is the role of the facilitator to judge when it is important to maintain a structure and organisation to the session, and when it might be appropriate to encourage more independent and spontaneous work from the group members.

The simplest way of engaging the group members is to ask direct questions at each stage of the exercise. These should be general, and each question designed to move the exercise on. The phrasing of each stage should be such that it enables each member to either expand on the question, or respond to it directly. All the exercises that you use in your group should be directed towards shared experiences; anchor the piece of writing from a point at which everyone can enter and allow for different kinds of responses to the questions (some of which you may not have anticipated).

A simple structure for an exercise can be organised around a set of questions that are keyed into a central theme. The exercise can move outwards from a concrete situation to the more abstract questions of feeling, memory and emotion, an initially very ordinary situation can prompt extraordinary memories or flights of imagination. Alternatively, it is possible to structure an exercise that moves in stages from a broad general landscape or event to more specific details of memory or imagination. Visual prompts can help to stimulate memories and to promote an imaginative response to the exercise.

Exercises are at their most accessible when they ask the group to write from direct experience and about relatively recent events. In the early stages of a group, the exercises should require the minimum of personal disclosure, and thereafter, should always allow the writers the option of distancing themselves. As the group develops, it becomes possible to ask the members to disclose more about the past, address issues relating to childhood and expand more on their home or family circumstances. As the group members develop confidence in their writing, work with imaginary situations or more formal literary exercises can be undertaken, and they can also be invited to write from another person's point of view.

Whatever the theme or the scenario of the writing session, the basic questions and stages of any exercise are as follows:

1. What was the situation?

2. Why were you there? When did this happen?

3. What can you see around you? (This can be developed by involving the other senses.)

4. Who were you with, or were you alone? (It is important to include both options – you cannot assume the presence of friends or family when people may have been in a very lonely situation.)

5. How did you feel in this situation?

Finally:

A 'Finally' section allows room for the group members to add anything that they feel they have left unsaid, but would like to include. This can help to allay feelings of being too constrained by the structured nature of the writing exercise, and allows for a space in which to bring the piece of writing to a conclusion.

It is important to be very specific in your requirements of the group at each stage of the exercise – time can be wasted if the instructions for a given task are not made clear, and it can make group members anxious if they are not sure of what they are doing.

Creative Writing Books
(or Why This Book is Necessary)

The majority of creative writing handbooks currently available are written for those who already have some confidence in their writing ability, and who are prepared to take risks. This is by no means the case for those who are for whatever reason in a vulnerable state or crisis situation.

Much of the literary critical work which engages with issues of mental health is very pscychoanalytically focused, while psychoanalysis remains a method which requires more time and attention than mental health services are currently in a position to provide. Most of the books that we have included in this list are introductions to creative writing. Some of these can be recommended to those who want to develop their writing while they are still working in the group, while others are more appropriate to suggest once members have left the group and perhaps joined a more formal creative writing group. There are others which are a useful resource for facilitators, some of which will provide ideas for further work in creative writing groups and some of which are useful as theoretical and professional resources.

Useful books

This is by no means an exhaustive account of the literature currently available, and not all of these texts will be of use to your particular circumstances. They do, however, represent a range of material which we have found useful in framing our own ideas on creative writing and mental health, and some of them are very suggestive for ways of developing work with a creative writing group. Some are more suitable for recommending to group members who are prepared to strike out with writing on their own, or who are ready to move on to a more specialist creative writing group, while others can give you more ideas and ways of developing your work within your own group. These can also provide an opportunity for considering and reflecting on your own practice as a facilitator.

Carmel Bird, *Dear Writer: Advice to Aspiring Authors*

(London: Virago Press, 1990)

This is a readable and accessible guide book, neatly written in the form of letters to an aspiring writer. But, as the title implies, it is addressed to those who already see themselves as writers, and particularly as novelists or short-story writers, rather than to those who may only be beginning to express themselves on paper. It is a useful guide to recommend to any members of the group, and especially women, who undertake writing outside the group, or to anyone whose confidence within the group develops to such an extent that they would like to take their writing further.

Gillie Bolton, *The Therapeutic Potential of Creative Writing*

(London: Jessica Kingsley Publishers, 1999)

This is an intensely personal account of the author's own practice and experience as a creative writing tutor in a range of therapeutic contexts. Bolton, a poet, has worked with groups of doctors, teachers, nurses and social workers. It is important in reading this book to recognise that much of her group work may not be appropriate to creative writing groups less practised in self reflexivity. Bolton can tend towards the breathless in her enthusiasm for the benefits of creative writing, and her points can be whimsical and are not always sufficiently theorised; nonetheless, there are some moving examples of writing from groups that she has worked with, and some good ideas on how to begin and to develop writing that could be adapted for use in other kinds of group, although its recommendations should be handled with some care. Very much addressed to the reader as a writer, the book would work best as a professional resource.

Julia Casterton, *Creative Writing: A Practical Guide*

(Basingstoke: Macmillan, 1986)

A useful guide for those planning to take writing further than the group, this is however very much addressed to those who, in Casterton's words, 'feel compelled to write'. The exercises do assume a commitment to writing which may not be present in the members of your own group, but this is nonetheless a good book to recommend to group members who may be inspired to strike out on their own.

Dianne Doubtfire, *Creative Writing*

(London: Hodder and Stoughton, 1983)

An accessible and easily available book in the Teach Yourself series, this is again a book for those in the group who are thinking about taking their writing seriously and on their own terms, and is aimed at those who are considering taking it up professionally. As such, it is full of useful and straightforward advice, but may well be too ambitious for those who do not have professional aspirations.

Sigmund Freud, 'Creative writers and daydreaming'

(1908, In *The Penguin Freud Library Volume 14: Art and Literature.* Harmondsworth: Penguin, 1990)

This is *the* psychoanalytic essay on creative writing in which Freud explores the relation between creativity in writing and children's play. It is of direct relevance to creative writing workshops in mental health institutions (although Freud does tend to suggest that the writer is a special category of being) in that it suggests that writing and other forms of creative play offer a therapeutic means of ordering the world.

Alida Gersie and Nancy King, *Storymaking in Education and Therapy*

(London: Jessica Kingsley Publishers, 1990)

This is a valuable resource of myths and stories from all over the world, organised into thematic sections. Each section ends with suggestions for writing and drama activities associated with its themes, and many of these could be adapted for use in a creative writing group. The authors have also included questions which could form the basis of writing exercises, and notes for facilitators. Clearly informed by a Jungian understanding of a collective unconscious, the authors' own celebration of myth and mysticism can at times come to sound a bit neo-spiritual. Nonetheless, the richness of the stories is such that this collection is very suggestive and well worth investigating. There is a good appendix, with suggestions of other sources for stories.

Alice Glarden Brand, *Therapy in Writing: A Psycho-Educational Enterprise*

(Lexington: Gower, 1981)

A very academic book, based on a PhD thesis, this is quite a clinical and technical account of the use of creative writing as a tool in the psychology of education. Nonetheless, the introductory chapter on 'The uses of writing in psychotherapy' offers a useful historical account of changing attitudes towards creative writing in mental health in the American context. Some of the activities and exercises that Glarden employs with two of the children who were among the subjects of her own research are suggestive, and could be borrowed or adapted for use with adults.

Ben Knights, *The Listening Reader: Fiction and Poetry for Counsellors and Psychotherapists*

(London: Jessica Kingsley Publishers, 1995)

A resource for facilitators rather than for other members of a writing group, in its acknowledgement of the resources that are required of the mental health professional, this is written with a sensitivity to the concerns of just these people. Although this is a book for self and professional development, rather than of direct practical application, Knights also provides a list of topics and of related readings in fiction and poetry which could prove very useful for extending discussions of work produced in the group. It contains a very good reading list of related psychotherapeutic and literary theory. This is a book that is about reading rather than writing, particularly 'the ways in which reading imaginative texts may feed into professional listening'. While it is largely an argument that therapists and counsellors have much to learn from literature, it does offer suggestive accounts of ways of reading and of engaging with literary texts that are of direct relevance to those working in a mental health context.

Celia Hunt and Fiona Sampson, *The Self on the Page: Theory and Practice of Creative Writing in Personal Development*

(London: Jessica Kingsley Publishers, 1998)

A valuable collection of articles for professional tutors and facilitators who are concerned with the theoretical aspects of creative writing in a therapeutic context. The wide-ranging collection includes contributions from academics, professional writers and therapists (and from some who are combinations of all three). The experiences recounted and theorised here range from accounts of working with individuals to work with groups of students, those in hospices and other hospital contexts. Although very much an academic book (many of the essays here do assume a thorough familiarity with psychoanalytic language – particularly Jungian), there are some engaging accounts of practical work in creative writing workshops. If the first half of the book is concerned with experimental accounts of the therapeutic practice of creative writing, the second sets out to map the current state of theory in the relationship between creative writing and therapeutic discourse. The book is therefore both good in offering practical experience and ideas, and also a useful focus for professional self-reflexivity, and for considering the implications of your own practice in a creative writing group.

Robert De Maria and Ellen Hope Meyer, *A Contemporary Reader for Creative Writing*

(London: Harcourt Brace, 1994)

A source book for students and teachers of creative writing workshops, this is a collection of readings from contemporary writers designed to introduce aspects of the writer's craft. The range of genres and writers is too generalised for the purposes of a writing group in a mental health context, but may well inspire exercises for use with a group. There are some suggestions for writing assignments for students, but these are for the most part too specific or too academic to be directly useful in the context of mental health.

Barry Maybury, *Writers' Workshop: Techniques in Creative Writing*

(London: Batsford, 1979)

A book written for teachers and lecturers in education, this is full of stimulating ideas and exercises that could well be adapted for use in a mental health context. Although the exercises are devised for students, and could be too direct or challenging in the form that they stand here for use in a group in a psychiatric context, many of them are close to those in this book and give some good indications of how this work could be expanded and developed. Many of the wordplay exercises could be used directly, while other suggestions could be broken down and structured for use in a more directed session. It is also a book that will encourage group members to explore outside creative groups, and give them a sense of the kind of work that may be expected. Very useful if inspiration runs dry!

Morris R. Morrison, *Poetry as Therapy*

(New York: Human Sciences Press, 1987)

This is a collection of essays based on a conference held in America in 1984. There are papers here from psychiatrists, psychotherapists, academics in literature, educational psychologists and counsellors. As such, it represents a broad account of professional experiences of the use of creative writing in a range of institutions, from colleges, schools and prisons as well as mental health institutions. There are also essays on work with adolescents and the elderly. This is a very encouraging collection, in that all the papers act as a reassurance of the value and importance of creative writing in therapeutic practice.

Matthew Sweeney and Ken Smith, *Beyond Bedlam*

(London: Anvil Press, 1998)

An inspirational collection of recent poetry, all concerned with aspects of mental health. Many of the poets are themselves users or ex-users of the mental health system; in the words of the editors (themselves poets), these are poems written by 'those who visit that wild country and return'. There are many ways in which this collection could be used, many of the poems could be adapted into exercises (see Chapter 11 for suggestions on how to model exercises from poetic ideas). The collection is in itself a demonstration of the value of creative writing in transforming and mediating the experience of mental distress, and is a valuable and encouraging volume to suggest to those group members who may be taking up poetry on their own.

Sue Thomas, *Creative Writing: A Handbook for Workshop Leaders*

(Nottingham: University of Nottingham Department of Adult Education, 1995)

Written by a creative writing tutor who has taught in schools, universities and in adult education, this is an extremely useful book, with workshop sessions that are often very close to the exercises in this book. Written for the tutors of adult education groups, the exercises are very clear and straightforward and therefore appropriate for use in other contexts. The handbook includes a set of essays by teachers of creative writing, which offer useful insights into how others run writing groups.

Useful Organisations

There are a great many organisations dedicated to the promotion of creative writing, and some which are specifically concerned with the relationship of mental health and writing. Some of these are organisations that are useful to recommend to group members who may be leaving the group and who want to move on to develop their writing in another context; others are useful supports for the facilitators of creative writing workshops, and may well be interested in the work that you are doing in your own institution.

Do check the addresses of these groups – these were the addresses current at the time of publication, but we cannot guarantee them to have remained the same.

Association of Occupational Therapists in Mental Health, 120 Wilton Road, London SW1V 1JZ

The Association of Occupational Therapists in Mental Health promotes support, communication and the exchange of information among Occupational Therapists in the field. Although not directly concerned with creative writing, it can provide support, and offers a means of exchanging and disseminating information about your work. It publishes a newsletter and holds specialist study days and conferences.

Centerprise Literature Development Project, 136–138 Kingsland High Street, London E8 2NS

Based in East London, and originally concerned with encouraging writing and publishing in the local community, Centerprise now offers a wide range of creative writing courses, events, advice and information. It has two strands, the Black Literature Development Project (BDLP) and the New Writing Development Project (NWDP). The BLDP specifically provides for writers of African and Asian descent, while the NWDP is open to anyone. It also provides programmes for particular groups, including those with disabilities, lesbians and gay men.

If your group is based in or near London, Centerprise is a valuable resource, and its weekend courses and workshops, and readings and events, could provide a useful transition for members who are considering writing more seriously. It is also a venue for outings for the group and provides lists of events.

LAPIDUS (The Association for the Literary Arts in Personal Development),
c/o The Poetry Society, 22 Betterton Street, London WC2

A group made up of creative writers, mental health practitioners and users of the mental health services, this organisation is dedicated to the promotion of creative writing as a tool in the development of mental health. This is an organisation that has many members who work in mental health contexts, and some who are researching the benefits of creative writing for mental health. They may well be interested in the work that you are doing.

NAWE (The National Association of Writers in Education),
PO Box 1, Sheriff Hutton, York YO6 7YU

A group for teachers and lecturers rather than for mental health professionals, NAWE is nonetheless a very useful source of contacts and ideas, and encourages links between writers and the community. They run annual conferences, issue a magazine, *Writing in Education*, and can provide speakers and professional writers who will run workshops.

SHAPE Network,
c/o ITHACA, Unit 1, St John Fisher School, Sandy Lane West, Blackbird Leys, Oxford OX4 5LD

The Shape Network is a federation of independent arts organisations which works to increase access to the arts for groups of people who are often excluded. Shape emerged out of regional groups and services which came together into a National Shape network in 1986. Its role is to share information, advise and support, and to lobby on arts and disability issues nationally. The Network has an Executive Committee, of which over half the membership must be recruited from user groups.

Shape's programmes include arts projects in arts venues and in institutional and community settings; it organises exhibitions, publications, performances, festivals and ticket schemes. It also offers support and training for artists with disabilities, sets up conferences and seminars, and offers advice and information services.

Survivor's Poetry,
34 Osnaburgh Street, London NW1 3ND

Survivor's Poetry is an organisation that offers writing workshops across the country which are specifically designed for those who have, in the words of their leaflet: 'a current or past experience of psychiatric hospitals, recipients of ECT, tranquillisers and other medication, users of counselling and therapy services, survivors of sexual abuse, child abuse, and other survivors who have empathy with our experience.' Survivor's Poetry publishes collections of work from its members, and organises readings. It would be a particularly useful contact for group members who have been users of the mental health system and who want to develop or promote their work outside of a hospital environment.

Worker's Educational Association (WEA)
Temple House, 17 Victoria Park Square, Bethnal Green,
London E3 9PB

The WEA runs adult education classes nationally, and these often include creative writing groups and writing workshops. To find out about local groups and their regional offices, contact the national office. A local evening class in creative writing can often be the best place to refer members of the group who have gone beyond what your own group can offer, and for those who have recovered sufficiently to want to make outside contacts. An evening class in a familiar subject can often be a very positive transition from a protected environment into the outside world.

The Authors

Deborah Philips teaches in the Department of Arts at Brunel University. She wrote her PhD on Henry James, and has written on popular culture. She is the co-author, with Ian Haywood, of *Brave New Causes* (Cassell 1998). She runs a creative writing group at St Charles Hospital, West London.

Liz Linington trained as an occupational therapist at Brunel University. She has worked in a variety of mental health settings around central London, and currently specialises in psychiatric rehabilitation. She has travelled extensively and has special interest in the use of therapy in cross-cultural psychiatry.

Debra Penman obtained her degree in English and American Studies from Hull University and then trained as an occupational therapist at St Loyes College, Exeter. She has since worked in a variety of specialisms and is currently working in a day centre in Shoreditch for people with HIV/AIDS.

References

Barthes, R. (1977) *Image/Music/Text.* London: Fontana.

Benson, G. (1987) 'Creative writing'. In G. Lee (ed) *The Creative Tree: Active Participation in the Arts for People who are Disadvantaged.* Salisbury: Michael Russell.

Benson, G., Chernaik, J. and Herbert, C. (eds) (1996) *Poems on the Underground,* Anniversary Edition. London: Cassell.

Cadman, E., Chester, G. and Pivot, A. (1981) *Rolling Our Own: Women as Printers, Publishers and Distributors.* London: Minority Press.

Casterton, J. (1986) *Creative Writing: A Practical Guide.* Basingstoke: Macmillan.

Cope, W. (1988) *Does She Like Word-Games?* London: Anvil Press Poetry.

Craig, W.J. (ed) (1972) *The Oxford Shakespeare: Complete Works.* Oxford: Oxford University Press.

Eagleton, T. (1996) *Literary Theory: An Introduction.* Oxford: Blackwell.

Freud, S. (1908) 'Creative writers and daydreaming'. In (1990) *The Penguin Freud Library, Volume 14: Art and Literature.* Harmondsworth: Penguin.

Gardner, H (ed) (1972) *The New Oxford Book of English Verse.* Oxford: Oxford University Press.

Glarden Brand, A. (1981) *Therapy in Writing: A Psycho-Educational Enterprise.* Lexington: Gower.

Hughes, T. (1975) *Season Songs.* London: Faber & Faber.

Kaminsky, M. (1987) 'Voices from within the process'. In M.R. Morrison (ed) *Poetry as Therapy.* New York: Human Sciences Press.

Laplanche, J. and Pontalis, J.B. (1988) *The Language of Psychoanalysis.* London: Karnac Books.

Lauer, R. and Goldfield, M. (1970) 'Creative Writing in Group Therapy'. *Psychotherapy: Theory, Research and Practice* 7, 4, 248–52.

Lee, G. (ed) (1987) *The Creative Tree: Active Participation in the Arts for People who are Disadvantaged.* Salisbury: Michael Russell.

Morrison, M.R. (ed) (1987) *Poetry as Therapy.* New York: Human Sciences Press.

Richards, I.A. (1929) *Practical Criticism: A Study of Literary Judgement.* London: Kegan Paul.

Rogers, T. (1987) *The Poems of Rupert Brooke: A Centenary Edition.* London: Black Swan.

Stegner, W. (1988) 'On the teaching of creative writing'. In E.C. Latham (ed) *Responses to a Series of Questions.* Hanover, NH: University Press of New England.

Pennar, M. (trans.) (1988) *Taliesin Poems.* Llanerch: Llanerch Enterprises.

Worpole, K. (1984) *Reading by Numbers: Contemporary Publishing and Popular Fiction.* London: Comedia.

Subject Index

Achievement 105–6
Admiration 80
age 28
Animals 55–6
appreciation, literary
  forms 19
Association of
  Occupational
  Therapists in Mental
  Health 135
audiences 33–4
awareness, of others 18

beginnings 45–51
Beyond Bedlam 134
Blind date 103
Bonfires 113–14
books, useful 129–34
Boredom 71–2
boundaries, professional
  23–4
Building 101–2

Cats/dogs 61
Celebrations 114–15
Centerprise Literature
  Development Project
  135
changes 85–8
Children's books 62–3
Christmas 112
Cinema 62
class differences 28
Clothes 54
Collective fairy tale 51

collective poems 30
Colours 49–50
community, sense of 17
concentration 18
confidentiality, writing
  groups 17, 20, 32
Consequences 47–8
*Contemporary Reader for
  Creative Writing, A*
  133
*Creative Writers and
  Daydreaming* 131
Creative Writing 131
*Creative Writing: A
  Handbook for
  Workshop Leaders*
  134–5
*Creative Writing: A
  Practical Guide* 130
cultural differences 27–8

Day out, A 56
*Dear Writer: Advice to
  Aspiring Authors* 130
Dens 66–7
Dinner party 82
discussions, about work
  23, 34
Does she like 120
drama 30–1

empathy 22, 77–84
endings 85–8
environmental awareness
  18
ethnic differences 27–8
evaluation, group
  experiences 34–6
Evoking the Past 61

exercises
  beginnings 45–51
  changes and endings
    85–8
  empathy 77–84
  general themes 42–3,
    109–15
  guidelines 125–7
  imagined worlds
    89–96
  introductory work
    53–6
  literary form, exploring
    117–24
  memories 57–76
  opening up 97–107
  warm-up 25, 39–44

facilitators, role of 22–3
Famous people 93–4
Favourite places 59–60
Favourite things 54–5
feedback 34
feelings, expression of
  16–17
Fireplace 64–5
Fireworks 112–13
First day at school 70
First drink 68–9
First love 67–8
First meeting, A 80–1
First time 75–6
Flowers 79–80
folk tales, Propp's
  analysis 51
Found poem 43
Friends and enemies
  73–4
Fruit 48

Games 59
Garden 100–1
general themes 42–3, 109–15
Getting to the group 53–4
Goodbyes 87–8
Group poem 43–4
guidelines, for exercises 125–7

haiku 121
Haunts 98–9
Hospital 70–1
House 100

I am and I like 41
I have been 85–6
I'd like to be 42
Ideal me 107
imagined worlds 89–96
Important people 84
interpretations 23, 34
introductions
    exercises 40–1
    writing groups 31–2
introductory work 53–6
Inventions 95–6
Irritation 74
Island 90–1

Jewellery 78
Journey 58–9

Landscape 46–7
LAPIDUS (The Association for the Literary Arts in Personal Development) 136

Listening Reader, The: Fiction and Poetry for Counsellors and Psychotherapists 132
literacy 21
literary forms 28–31
    appreciation of 19
    exploring 43–4, 117–24

Making history 92
Martian 118–19
Me 42
Media 42
membership, writing groups 20–1
memories 57–76
Moods 102–3
Music 110–11
Myself 104–5

Name game 40
NAWE (The National Association of Writers in Education) 136
negative capability 22

Object 43, 50
opening up exercises 41–2, 97–107
organisation, writing groups 31
organisations, useful 135–7
Other people 79

painful feelings
    confronting 26
    exercises 69–76

poetry 19
Paradise 94–5
Park 91
Pastimes 65–6
Perfect day 60
performance, in public 36–7
phantasies, expression of 17, 37
poetry 29–30
    exercises 120–4
    painful feelings 19
Poetry as Therapy 134
Politics 114
Pop stars 67
Portraits 45–6
positive memories 57–69
Presents 81–2
Problem page 82–3
professional boundaries 23–4
prompt cards 20
Propp, Vladimir 51
prose 28–9
public display, of work 36–7

Relaxation 57–8
religious beliefs 27
reminiscence 17–18
Room 89–90, 99
Rose bush 101
rules, writing groups 32–3

Safe place 104
Saved 43
Scents 111

Seasons 42, 86
Self on the Page, The:
Theory and Practice of
Creative Writing in
Personal Development
132–3
self-esteem 18
self-expression 14, 37
sessions, group
approaching 24–7
structure of 33
Seven joys of autumn,
The 121–2
sexuality 28
SHAPE Network 136–7
sharing, of work 33–4
Shopping 77–8
skills, writing 19
Someone else's eyes
83–4
Sonnet 122–4
Special knowledge 41–2
spontaneity, in writing
25
Station 103–4
Story wheel 48–9
Storymaking in Education
and Therapy 131
Stranded on a train 72
Strengths 106
Summertime 110
Surnames 43
Surprises 41
Survivor's Poetry 137
sympathy 22

Taliesin 118
Teachers 72–3

Television/radio 63–4
Theatre 93
therapeutic benefits, of
writing 13–16
Therapeutic Potential of
Creative Writing, The:
Writing Myself 130
therapy, writing as
16–19
Therapy in Writing: A
Psycho-Educational
Enterprise 132
These I have loved
119–20
Things I find difficult 76
Threat 74–5
time, orientation in 18
Time machine 91–2
Toys 65
True or False? 41
trust, writing groups 17,
21, 32
Twenty years on 87
Typical day 98

unsatisfying reality 38
Utopia 95

Walk 109–10
warm-up exercises 25,
39–44
Words 42
work, sharing 33–4
Worker's Educational
Association (WEA)
137
Writers' Workshop:
Techniques in Creative
Writing 133

writing
therapeutic benefits
13–16
as therapy 16–19
writing groups 17
facilitators 22–3
introductions 31–2
members 20–1
organisation 31
requirements for
19–20
rules 32–3
sessions
approaching 24–7
structure of 33
writing skills 19

Author Index

Barthes, R. 24
Benson, G. 23

Cadman, E., Chester, G.
    and Pivot, A. 15
Casterton, J. 16, 29
Cope, W. 41, 120
Craig, W.J. 123

Eagleton, T. 51

Freud, S. 14, 17, 37

Gardner, H. 123
Glarden Brand, A. 16

Hughes, T. 122

Kaminsky, M. 15

Laplanche, J. and
    Pontalis, J.B. 37
Lauer, R. and Goldfield,
    M. 14

Morrison, M.R. 16, 17

Pennar, M. 118

Raine, C. 118
Richards, I.A. 29
Rogers, T. 60, 119

Stegner, W. 22, 33, 37

Worpole, K. 15